nursery knits

Zoë Mellor
nursery knits

25 easy-knit designs for clothes,
toys and decorations

hamlyn

This book is dedicated to
Nims, Toby and Kitty.

First published in Great Britain in 2005
by Hamlyn,
a division of Octopus Publishing Group Ltd
2–4 Heron Quays, London E14 4JP

ISBN 0 600 61121 3
EAN 9780600611219

A CIP catalogue record for this book is
available from the British Library

Printed and bound in China

10 9 8 7 6 5 4 3 2 1

contents

introduction

Having recently opened a new children's wear shop, I realize how difficult it is to find lovely things for children's bedrooms. The Party Flags (see page 82) are such a great hit with my own children that my daughter has them hanging in her bedroom. The Play Cubes (see page 78) are great for children to sit on as well as to play with and will fit into any colour scheme.

The other favourite of mine is My First Teddy (see page 60). He is just the kind of teddy to become a treasured favourite and he's really easy to make. I have included some luxurious yarns, whilst keeping the patterns simple and uncluttered for quick results. The Angel Dress (see page 95) is perfect for a special occasion. You can always knit it in white for a christening or in a shocking pink for a striking party dress.

In writing this book, I really wanted to challenge some of the stereotypical views of knitwear and I hope I have inspired you to knit items that are more traditionally made from fabric. After all, knitting is just another fabric and its soft feel only makes you want to touch it more. I hope you enjoy knitting these designs as much as I have enjoyed dreaming them up!

Happy knitting!

Zoë Mellor

yarns

When creating knits for children it is important to place equal emphasis on the comfort of the yarns and to the allover look of the outfit. My own two children are always in my mind when I am designing and I stick to what would suit them. Think about the child you're knitting for and choose colours that would suit them.

Designing for children has fewer restraints than designing for adults, as children seem happier to wear brighter shades and enjoy a sense of fun in their clothing. Be sure to take the opportunity to try out different colours from the ones I have used. You'll get a lot of satisfaction knitting up swatches while playing with colour schemes.

Colour has such a strong effect on a design – the same design can look so totally different made in a different set of shades – for example with the Party Flags (see page 82). Experiment with colours that catch your eye. Adding your own touches to designs will make you treasure them even more.

yarn types

It is a good idea to buy the yarn brand recommended in my knitting patterns. I will have chosen the yarn because its weight and texture perfectly suit that particular design. Since comfort is a top priority for babies' and toddlers' knits, cotton yarns feature prominently in my designs. They are soft enough for children's sensitive skin, aren't itchy and are ideal to wear all year round – warm in winter and cool in summer.

Consider the qualities of the yarn you're going to use before starting your knit. Synthetics may be easy to wash, but natural fibres maintain their elegance for many years and get even better with age. Tiny tot knits in natural fibres can be passed down to a new sibling and still look good. Here are the pros of my favourite yarns – wool, cotton, silk and cashmere:

wool is traditionally associated with knitting. It is springier than cotton and is warm and great for cold weather. Taking dyes well, it comes in masses of good colours. Some wool yarns, such as Botany, are softer to the touch than others, so pick them carefully.

cotton allows your skin to breathe. It is cooler than wool and non-itchy, making it ideal as an all-year-round yarn. As cotton is not as elastic as wool, maintain a fairly tight tension (gauge) when knitting it up so that your knit holds its shape properly.

silk is a natural yarn with a luxurious, smooth feel and a gentle sheen. It's great for special projects as its subtle sheen really adds a wow factor.

cashmere is amazingly soft to the touch. Like wool it holds its shape well when knitted. Cashmere does have to be washed with care so it may be better used in items for special occasions. It is ideal for children with very sensitive skin.

yarn and dye lots

Yarn is dyed in batches and dye lots can vary greatly. It is essential to check the dye lot number on your yarn label to make sure that you use the same dye lot for the main colour of what you are knitting, otherwise you run the risk of your knit being unintentionally stripy. If it is not possible to get all the yarn you need for your main colour from the same dye lot, use the odd ball for the ribbed borders. The raised texture of the ribbing disguises the colour discrepancy. For colours dotted around

the design, variations in dye lots won't matter as long as they aren't touching each other.

substituting yarn

If you want to knit with different yarns from those specified in the patterns, please remember to think about the stitch size and the weight of the yarn. A yarn might knit up to the right number of stitches and rows to the centimetre (inch) but the resulting fabric may be so heavy that it pulls your design out of shape. Before you use a different yarn, I recommend that you knit a tension (gauge) square to check the stitch size and then see if you like the feel of the fabric.

Cotton yarn is heavier than wool and less elastic when knitted, so always check the tension before you change yarns from those stated in the pattern.

colour

Many of the patterns in this book involve colour knitting techniques. If the design is not a Fair Isle and the colours are in blocks, use the intarsia method of colour knitting. An example of intarsia knitting is the motif on the Kitten and Puppy Sweaters (see page 22) or Zoo Toy Bag (see page 75). When working intarsia, do not carry the yarn across the back of the work; instead use a separate ball of yarn for each isolated area of colour. Where a block of colour is small, you can use a long length of yarn or a small amount wound around a bobbin. The intarsia method prevents the knitting from becoming too bulky and also avoids pulling and distortion across the motif. When changing from one colour to another, twist the yarns around each other to prevent holes from forming. If you still see holes at the colour-change points, try twisting the yarn twice to pull the colours even closer together.

When knitting a Fair Isle design, strand the yarns across the back of the work, picking them up and dropping them as they are needed. Make sure that you don't pull the yarns too tightly, as this will distort the shape of the knitting and make the garment narrower than it should be. The back of the Fair Isle should not have very long loops, as this type of design is repetitive and the yarn colours repeat every few stitches. If the loops are too long they can get caught and pulled by tiny fingers.

tailored to fit your baby

Knitting patterns always give the finished knitted measurement of the garment around the chest, from top to bottom, and the sleeve seam. A good way to check that you are choosing the right size is to match these measurements to a knit that you know is just right for your tiny tot. If in doubt, pick the next size up, as the child will soon grow into it.

Once you've chosen the right size in which to knit the pattern, all you need to do is make sure your knitting turns out the way it should. Tension (gauge) is probably the most important thing to get right when beginning to knit a pattern or even to design knitwear. Many knitters get so carried away with wanting to get knitting that they don't bother to knit a test square. Please do bother – it can make the difference between a professional-looking garment and a badly fitted garment.

Tension (gauge) is simply the measurement of the tightness or looseness of the knitted fabric. On most yarn labels the recommended tension (gauge) is given in terms of the number of stitches and the number of rows over 10cm (4in) of stocking (stockinette) stitch.

Use the needle size specified in the pattern as well, at least for your first attempt at a test swatch. Generally, the finer the yarn, the smaller the needle size used for it, and the thicker the yarn, the bigger the needles. I tend to use medium-weight yarns because I like to see my knitting grow quite quickly.

tension (gauge) test

To measure your tension (gauge), first knit a swatch at least 15cm (6in) square. This gives you plenty of room to accurately measure the number of stitches and rows over 10cm (4in). To stop the edges curling when you measure it, flatten the swatch on a table top or pin it to your ironing board until it is flat. Steam press if necessary (see Blocking, page 17).

Checking stitch tension (gauge)

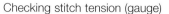
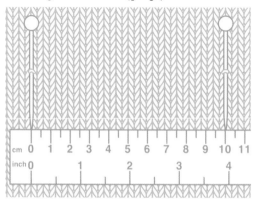

Checking row tension (gauge)

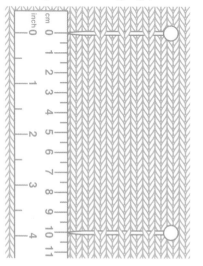

To check stitch tension (gauge), measure with a ruler and use pins to mark 10cm (4in) widthways across your swatch; always measure from the centre of your swatch. Count the number of stitches between the pins. To check row tension (gauge), do the same, but lengthways. If the number of stitches/rows is greater than that stated in the pattern, your stitch size is too small and you need to use larger needles. If the number of stitches/rows is fewer than in the pattern, your stitch size is too big and you need to use smaller needles. Keep doing test squares, changing needle size as required, until you get the right tension (gauge).

When you actually begin to knit your garment, you may find that with more stitches on the needles you are knitting more tightly or loosely. If so, check your tension (gauge) on the actual garment, and adjust the needle size if necessary.

sizing

Knitters often ask me if I can give them instructions for the next size up of a design. This is not always a quick calculation to make and I am rarely able to supply such tailor-made patterns. However, as a general rule knitters can make these amendments to my patterns themselves without too much trouble.

altering length

To change the length of a garment, you need to add more rows. The pattern tension (gauge) will tell you how many rows you need for 10cm (4in). Simply divide that number by 10 to find out how many extra rows will make 1cm (or divide that number by 4 to find out how many extra rows will make an extra inch). Measure the child you are making the garment for to see how much longer you need to make it. For example, if you need to make the design 2.5cm (1in) longer, just multiply your centimetre calculation by 2.5 (or multiply your inch calculation by 1).

altering width

Change the width of a garment in the same way that you would change the length – use the number of stitches per 10cm (4in) to calculate how many stitches to add.

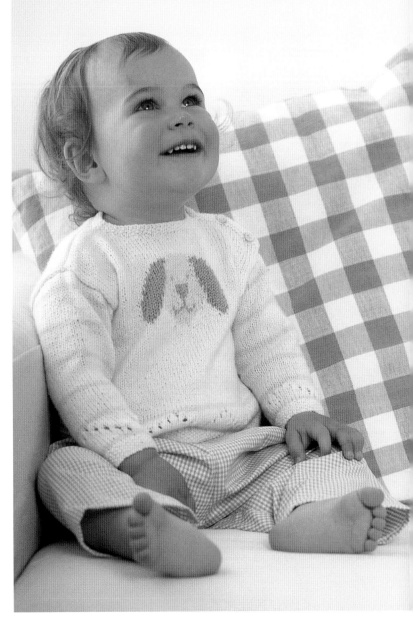

a simple reminder

When altering the lengths and widths of my knitting, I find it handy to start out by jotting down the following:

    1cm (or inch) up = X rows
    1cm (or inch) across = X stitches

Fill in the X's with your calculations and refer back to these notes whenever you need to.

finishing

Finishing your knit well is essential for achieving a successful and professional-looking item. Although the processes involved can be time-consuming, it is time well spent, for careless finishing can spoil the effect of even the most beautiful knitting.

yarn ends

The number of yarn ends left when an item is completed can be astonishing – and daunting. Many knitters I know find the first stage in finishing – sewing in yarn ends – a tedious task. They would rather start knitting their next project than finish the job in hand. Over the years I have grown fonder of sewing in ends; it can be quite therapeutic! A quick way I have discovered is first to weave a darning needle through the back of the knitting and then thread the end through. This prevents short ends from slipping out of the needle as you weave.

backstitch

Backstitch is good for sewing in sleeves or for tidying edges with lots of colour joins.

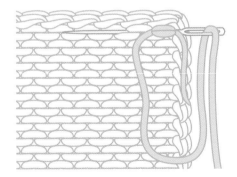

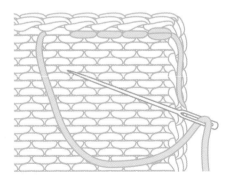

1 With right sides together, secure the seam with a starting stitch. Bring the sewing needle through both pieces of knitting, making your first stitch about 1cm (⅜in) in size.

2 Then loop back to where the yarn came out of your stitch and bring the needle out a little past the end of the last stitch. Continue like this, taking the needle backward and forward with each stitch.

1 With the right sides facing you, insert your blunt-ended sewing needle into the knitting between the first and second stitches on the first row of the seam.

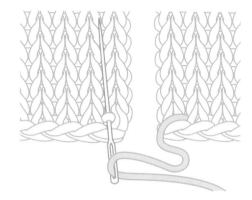

2 Then insert the needle in the other piece, in the centre of the second stitch in from the edge. Link the sides in a zigzag manner as shown below.

3 On garter stitch, work through the lower loop on one edge, then through the upper loop of the corresponding stitch on the other edge.

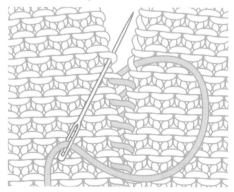

mattress stitch

Sewing perfect seams is very important when finishing an item. Mattress stitch is the most basic seaming technique. I use it probably more than any other method as it produces a totally invisible and straight seam. It is especially useful when seaming a striped item. If backstitch is used, which entails pinning the pieces together with right sides facing, stripes can move out of alignment, whereas mattress stitch, which avoids pinning and is worked on the right side, will achieve a perfect match.

blocking

Blocking, or pressing, your pieces of knitting before
sewing the seams gives a more professional finish, as
the edges will be flatter and not curl up. Always check
the yarn label for temperatures and to see if you can
press directly onto your knitting. Most of the yarns I
have chosen can be pressed, but if your yarn contains
acrylic it may not be suitable for pressing.

   To block your knitting, carefully pin each piece face
down on a flat surface – I find the ironing board ideal.
While pinning the pieces, gently nudge them into the
desired shape without pulling the stitches too tightly.
Then lightly press or steam the knitted fabric (on the
back of the work) until it is flat. If you steam your
knitting, remember to let it dry out completely before
removing the pins.

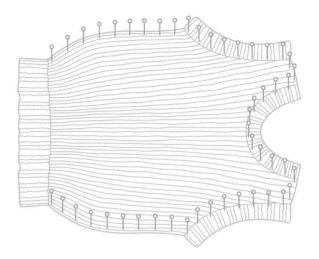

edgings

The simpler the shape and design of the item, the
more perfect your finishing touches have to be. I
love simple contrasting edges that give a garment
that little special detail. The tassels on the Head
Honcho Poncho (see page 111), make a fun edging
and give it that Mexican feel. The picot edge on the
Angel Dress (see page 95) adds a sweet detail. It's
these finishing touches that make all the difference.

Once your knitted garment is blocked and stitched
together, you are ready to sew on the buttons if
there are any. Choose interesting buttons for the
perfect personal touch, but try not to let them take
your design over – sometimes 'less is more'.
Usually, the simpler the design, the more detailed
the buttons can be, and the more complicated the
knitted fabric, the simpler the buttons should be.
Take your finished knitting with you when buying
your buttons so you can test the effect different
buttons have on the garment.

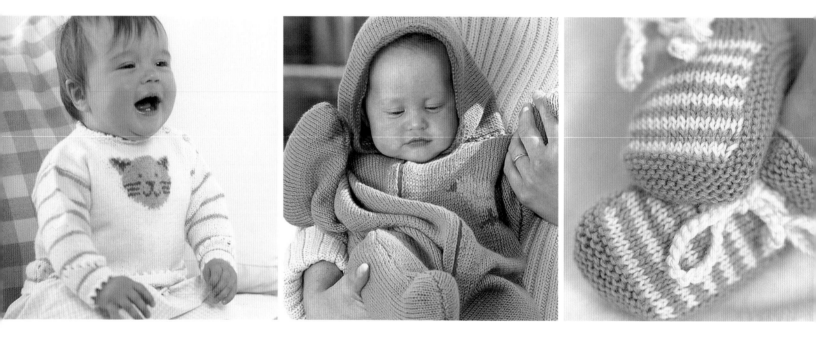

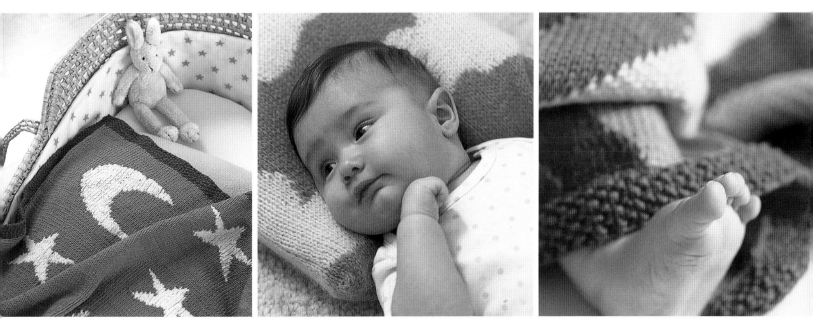

new baby snugglers

kitten and puppy sweaters

In gentle pastel colourways, these knits look sweet on babies. The soft yarn will keep them warm and cosy on cool days.

materials

Kitten: 2(2:3) 50g/1¾oz balls of Jaeger *Baby Merino* 4 ply in main colour **M** (ivory/Pearl 103) and 1 50g/1¾oz of Jaeger *Matchmaker* 4 ply in **A** (pale pink/Magnolia 124) and **B** (dark pink/Princess 126)

Puppy: 2(2:3) 50g/1¾oz balls of Jaeger *Baby Merino* 4 ply in main colour **M** (white/White 102) and 1 50g/1¾oz ball in **A** (pale green/Mint 101) and **B** (green/Spearmint 118)

Pair each of 2¾mm(US 2) and 3¼mm(US 3) knitting needles

3 buttons

sizes

to fit

3–6	6–9	9–12	mths

actual measurements

chest

51	55	61	cm
20	21¾	24	in

length to shoulder

25	28	30	cm
9¾	11	12	in

sleeve

15	17	19	cm
6	6¾	7½	in

tension/gauge

28 sts and 36 rows to 10cm/4in over st-st using 3¼mm(US 3) needles

abbreviations

alt alternate; **cm** centimetre(s); **cont** continue; **dec** decreas(e)(ing); **inc** increas(e)(ing); **in** inch(es); **k** knit; **k2tog** knit next 2 sts together; **mm** millimetre(s); **p** purl; **p2tog** purl next 2 sts together; **PM** place marker; **rem** remain(ing); **RS** right side; **st(s)** stitch(es); **st-st** stocking/stockinette stitch; **yo (yarn over needle)** take yarn over right needle to make a st; **yrn (yarn round needle)** wrap yarn around right needle from front to back and to front again between needles to make a st; **WS** wrong side

note

When working from chart, use separate small balls of yarn for each colour area and twist yarns at colour change to avoid holes.

NEW BABY SNUGGLERS

back

**With 2¼mm(US 2) needles and M, cast on 73(79:87) sts.

1st row (moss/seed st) K1, *p1, k1, rep from * to end.

Rep this row 6 times more.

Change to 3¼mm(US 3) needles and B.

1st row (WS) P.

2nd row K.

3rd row Change to M and p 1 row.

Now work lace panel as folls:

1st row (RS) K4(7:11), *yo, k2tog, k14: rep from * ending last rep k3(6:10).

2nd, 4th, 6th and 8th rows (WS) P.

3rd row K2(5:9), *yo, k2tog, k2, yo, k2tog, k10: rep from * ending last rep k1(4:8).

5th row K8(3:7), *yo, k2tog, k6: rep from * ending last rep k7(2:6).

7th row K10(1:1), yo, k2tog, [k2, yo, k2tog] 1(0:1) time, *k10, yo, k2tog, k2, yo, k2tog; rep from * to last 9(12:0) sts, k9(10:0), [yo, k2tog] 0(1:0) time.

9th row K12(15:3), *yo, k2tog, k14; rep from * ending last rep k11(14:2).

Change to A and work 2 rows.

Change to M.**

Beg with a p (WS) row, cont in M only and work 33(39:43) rows st-st, so ending with a p row.

shape armholes

Cast/bind off 4(5:6) sts at beg of next 2 rows. 65(69:75) sts.

Cont straight for 34(38:42) more rows, ending with a p row.

shape shoulders

Next row Cast/bind off 18(20:22) sts, k to end.

Next row K18(20:22) sts, turn, leaving rem 29(29:31) sts on a holder for back neck.

Knit 2 rows for button shoulder band.

Cast/bind off knitwise.

front

Work as given for Back from ** to **.

Beg with a p (WS) row, cont in M only and work 25(33:39) rows st-st.

Chart placement row (RS) K22(25:28), k across

29 sts of 1st row of chart, k22(25:29).

This row sets the position of the chart. Work 7(5:3) rows more in st-st, while keeping chart correct.

shape armholes

Keeping chart correct, cast/bind off 4(5:6) sts at beg of next 2 rows. 65(69:75) sts.

Cont in st-st until all 24 chart rows have been worked, then cont in M only and work 8(10:10) rows st-st, so ending with a p row.

shape neck

1st row (RS) K26 (28:30), turn and cont on these sts only, leaving rem sts on a spare needle.

2nd row Cast/bind off 3 sts (neck edge), p to end. 23(25:27) sts.

3rd–5th rows Work in st-st dec 1 st at neck edge. 20(22:24) sts.

6th–9th rows Work in st-st dec 1 st at neck edge on 7th and 9th rows. 18(20:22) sts.

3rd size only

Work 2 rows st-st.

all sizes

Next row K.

Work 6(6:4) rows.

Next row (make buttonholes) (RS) K5, yo, k2tog, k5(6:7), yo, k2tog, k4(5:6).

K 2 rows.

Cast/bind off knitwise.

With RS facing, slip 13(13:15) sts at centre front onto a holder, rejoin yarn to rem 26(28:30) sts, k to end.

2nd row P.

3rd row Cast/bind off 3 sts (neck edge), k to end.

4th–6th rows Work in st-st dec 1 st at neck edge. 20(22:24) sts.

7th–10th rows Work in st-st dec 1 st at neck edge on 7th and 9th rows. 18(20:22) sts.

3rd size only

Work 2(2:4) rows st-st.

Cast/bind off.

sleeves

With 3¼mm(US 3) needles and M, cast on 35(39:43) sts.

Work 7 rows in moss/seed st as given for Back.

Change to 3¼mm(US 3) needles and B.

1st row (WS) P.

2nd row K.

3rd row Change to M and p, inc 1 st at each end on 2nd and 3rd sizes only. 35 (41:45) sts.

Now work lace panel as follows:

1st row (RS) K1, (4:6), [yo, k2tog, k14] twice, yo, k2tog, k0(3:5).

2nd, 4th, 6th and 8th rows (WS) P.

3rd row K3(6:8), [yo, k2tog, k10, yo, k2tog, k2] twice, k0(3:5).

5th row Inc in 1st st, k4(7:9), [yo, k2tog, k6] 3 times, yo, k2tog, k3(6:8), inc in last st.

7th row K8(11:13), yo, k2tog, k2, yo, k2tog, k10, yo, k2tog, k2, yo, k2tog, k7(10:12).

9th row Inc in 1st st, k9(12:14), yo, k2tog, k14, yo, k2tog, k8(11:13), inc in last st.

Beg with a WS row, cont in st-st working stripes of 2 rows A and 10 rows M **while at the same time**, inc 1 st at each end of every foll 4th row until there are 55(59:63) sts.

Cont straight until sleeve measures 15(17:19)cm/6(6¾:7½)in from cast-on edge.

PM at each end of last row, then work a further 5(6:7) rows.

Cast/bind off.

moss/seed stitch neckband (puppy)

**Join right shoulder seam. With RS facing, 2¾mm(US 2) needle and M, pick up and k14(14:16) sts down buttonhole band and left front neck, k across 13(13:15) sts at centre front, pick up and k14(14:16) sts up right front neck, k across 29(29:31) sts at centre back, then pick up and k4 sts up button band edge. 74(74:82) sts.*

1st row *K1, p1, rep from * to end.

2nd row P1, k1, p1, yrn, p2tog, *k1, p1 rep from * to end.

Work 2 more rows in moss/seed st.**

Cast/bind off in moss/seed st.

picot neck edging (kitten)

Work as moss/seed st neckband from ** to **, then work picot cast/bind off edge as follows:

Cast/bind-off row (WS) Cast/bind off 3(3:5) sts, *slip st from right needle back onto left needle, cast on 2 sts, cast/bind off 5 sts, rep from * to end.

to finish

Work lace edgings (optional) before making up. With centre of cast/bind-off edge of sleeve to shoulder, sew sleeves into armholes with row ends above markers, sewn to cast/bind-off sts at underarm. Join side seams. Join sleeve seams unless working optional lace edge. Sew on buttons to match buttonholes.

optional lace sleeve edging (kitten)

With RS facing, 2¾mm(US 2) needle and M, pick up and k 35(39:43) sts along sleeve edge.

picot cast/bind-off edge

Cast/bind-off row (WS) Cast/bind off 5(3:4) sts, * slip st from right needle back onto left needle, cast on 2 sts, cast/bind off 5 sts, rep from * to end.

Join sleeve seam.

optional lace lower edging (kitten)

With RS facing, 2¾mm(US 2) needle and M, pick up and k73(79:87) sts from lower edge of front.

Cast/bind-off row (WS) Cast/bind off 3 sts, *slip st from right needle back onto left needle, cast on 2 sts, cast/bind off 5 sts, rep from * to end.

Repeat for back lower edge.

kitten motif

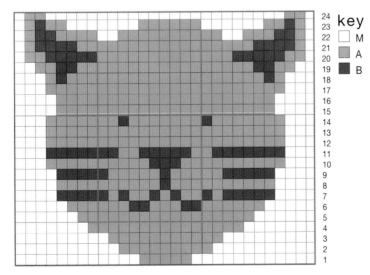

key
- ☐ M
- ▨ A
- ■ B

24
23
22
21
20
19
18
17
16
15
14
13
12
11
10
9
8
7
6
5
4
3
2
1

puppy motif

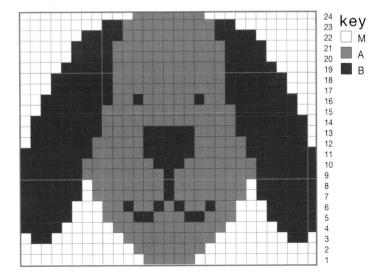

key
- ☐ M
- ▨ A
- ■ B

24
23
22
21
20
19
18
17
16
15
14
13
12
11
10
9
8
7
6
5
4
3
2
1

outdoor snuggle

This little snuggle is great for days out with your newborn baby, and the chick motif is cute for boys or girls. It fits over clothing and can be kept on in the buggy or carrier.

materials

6 50g/1¾oz balls of *Rowan Wool Cotton* in main colour **M** (pale green/Riviera 930), 1 50g/1¾oz ball of Jaeger *Baby Merino DK* in **A** (orange/Orange 234) and 1 ball in **B** (yellow/Gold 225)
Pair each of 3mm(US 2–3) and 3¾mm(US 5) knitting needles
Spare knitting needle
40cm/16in zip fastener to match orange (**A**)

size

to fit
0–3 mths

tension/gauge

23 sts and 32 rows to 10cm/4in over st-st using 3mm(US 2–3) needles

abbreviations

alt alternate; **beg** begin(ning); **cm** centimetre(s); **cont** continue; **dec** decreas(e)(ing); **foll(s)** follow(s)(ing); **inc** increas(e)(ing); **in** inch(es); **k** knit; **k2tog** knit next 2 sts together; **mm** millimetre(s); **p** purl; **p2tog** purl next 2 sts together; **patt** pattern; **rem** remain(ing); **RS** right side; **st(s)** stitch(es); **st-st** stocking/stockinette stitch

note

When working from chart, use separate small balls of yarn for each colour area and twist yarns at colour change to avoid holes.

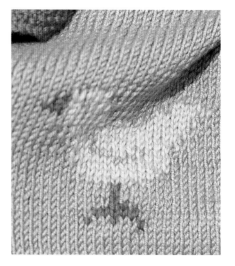

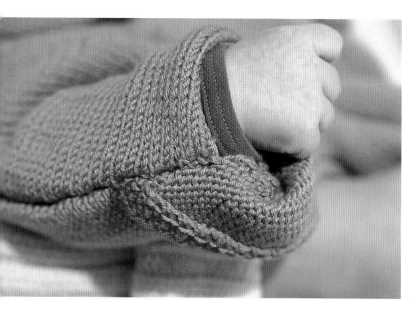

left front

Start at foot. With 3¾mm(US 5) needles and M, cast on 11 sts.

1st row K.
2nd row Cast on 3 sts, p to end. 14 sts.
3rd row Inc in first st, k to end. 15 sts.
4th–7th rows As 2nd–3rd rows. 23 sts.
8th row Cast on 2 sts, p to end. 25 sts.
9th row K.
10th–26th rows As 8th–9th rows. 43 sts.
27th row K2tog, k to end. 42 sts.
28th–31st rows As 8th–9th rows. 46 sts.
32nd row As 8th row. 48 sts. ##
33rd–94th rows Cont in st-st, dec 1 st at beg of 39th, 51st, 63rd, 75th and 87th rows. 43 sts.
shape arm
95th–106th rows Continue in st-st and cast on 2 sts beg each k row. 55 sts.
107th row Start motif in A, cast on 2 sts, k21, work 23 sts of 1st row of chart, k11. 57 sts.
108th row P11, work 2nd row of chart, p23.
109th–117th rows Cont casting on 2 sts at beg of every k row, and working motif. 67 sts.
118th–148th rows Work on st-st without shaping, completing motif.

shape shoulder and neck
149th row Dec, k to end. 66 sts.
150th row Cast/bind off 5 sts, p to end. 61 sts.
151st row Cast/bind off 3 sts, k to end. 58 sts.
152nd row Cast/bind off 4 sts, p to end. 54 sts.
153rd–156th row Cast/bind off 3 sts, work to end. 42 sts.
157th row Cast/bind off 3 sts, k to last 2 sts, k2tog. 38 sts.
158th row P2tog, p to end. 37 sts.
159th row Cast/bind off 3 sts, k to last 2 sts, k2tog. 38 sts. 33 sts.
160th row P.
161st row Cast/bind off 7 sts, k to last 2 sts, k2tog. 25 sts.
162nd–163rd row As 160th–161st row. 17 sts.
164th row P.
165th row Cast/bind off 7 sts, k to end. 10 sts.
166th row P.
Cast/bind off.

right front

Work as given for Left Front, reversing all shaping (an easy way to do this is to foll patt for Left Front but read p for k and k for p), and ignoring motif.

back

right back
Work to ## of Right Front and leave sts on spare needle.
left back
Work to ## of Left Front and cont as folls:
back
33rd row K48 from left back, cast on 1 st, k48 from right back. 97 sts.
34th–94th rows Dec each end of 39th, 51st, 63rd, 75th, 87th rows. 87 sts.
shape arms
95th–128th rows Cast on 2 sts, work to end. 155 sts.
129th–142nd rows Work in st-st without shaping.
shape shoulders
143rd–160th rows Cast/bind off 3 sts, work to end. 101 sts.

161st row Cast/bind off 7 sts, k31, cast/bind off 25 sts, k to end.
162nd row Cast/bind off 7 sts, work to end. 24 sts.
163rd row Cast/bind off 5 sts, work to end. 19 sts.
164th row Cast/bind off 7 sts, work to last 2 sts, dec 11 sts.
165th row Dec, work to end. 10 sts.
Cast/bind off.
Rejoin yarn to rem sts at neck edge and work 163rd to 166th rows.

hand flap

left hand
With 3¾mm(US 5) needles and M, cast on 3 sts and p 1 row.
2nd–14th row Working in st-st, cast on 2 sts beg of next and every alt row. 17 sts.
15th row P.
16th row Cast on 3 sts, k to end. 20 sts.
17th–31st row Work in st-st without shaping.
32nd–42nd row Cast/bind off 3 sts beg of next and every alt row. 5 sts.
43rd row P.
Cast/bind off.
right hand
Work as given for Left Hand, but reversing all shaping (work k as p and p as k).

edging
RS facing, with 3mm(US 2–3) needles and A, pick up and k33 sts along straight edges of flaps.
1st row *K1, p1, rep from * to end.
2nd row As 1st row.
Cast/bind off in moss/seed stitch.

hood
With 3mm(US 2–3) needles and A, cast on 101 sts and work 6 rows in moss/seed st.
Change to 3¾mm(US 5) needles and M, work in st-st until hood measures 16cm 6¼in, ending with a p row.

shape top of hood
1st row K50, cast/bind off 1 st, k50.
2nd row On 50 sts p48, p2tog. 49 sts.
3rd row K2tog, k to end. 48 sts.
4th and alt rows P.
5th row Cast/bind off 2 sts, k to end. 46 sts.
7th row As 5th row. 44 sts.
9th row Cast/bind off 4 sts, k to end. 40 sts.
11th row Cast/bind off 4 sts, k to end. 36 sts.
12th row P.
Cast/bind off.
Rejoin yarn to rem sts and work to match, reversing all shaping.

to finish
Weave in any loose ends. With RS together, pin hand flaps to back. With RS facing, pin fronts to back (front arm will overlap hand flap). Starting at neck edge, sew around garment (shoulder, hand, underarm, side seam, 1st leg, 2nd leg and back to neck). Sew centre back seam of hood. Pin hood to neck, starting and finishing 3 sts from centre front and sew into place. Insert zip fastener then join seam between bottom of zip fastener and crotch.

chick motif

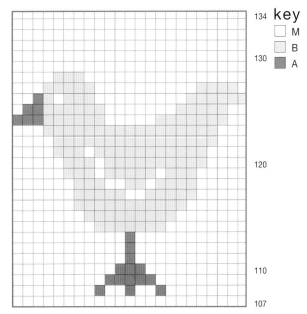

	key
☐	M
▨	B
▦	A

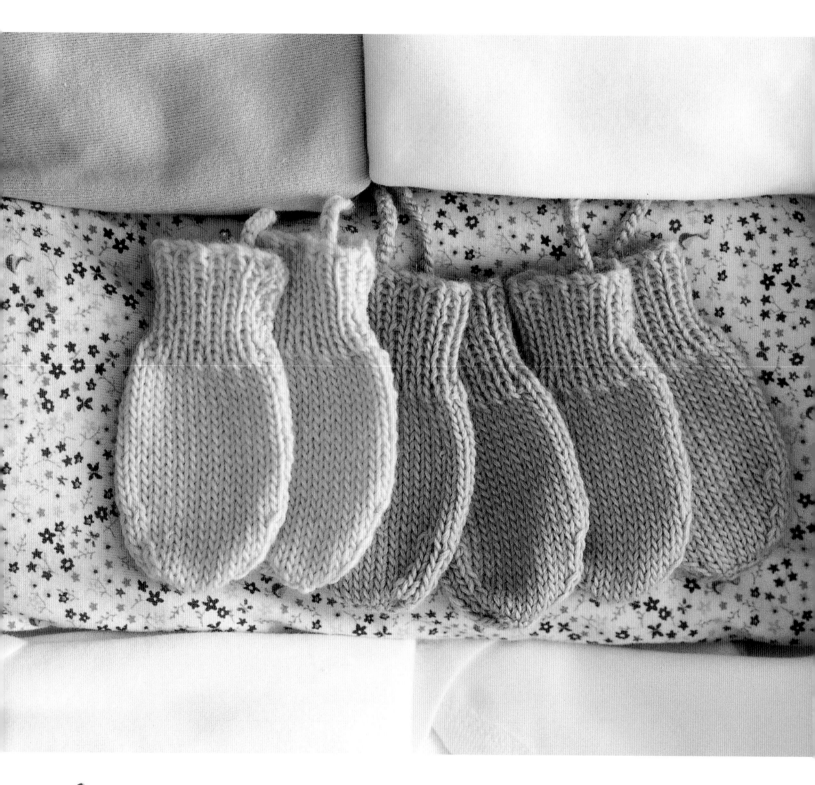

NEW BABY SNUGGLERS

mini mittens

These cashmere mittens are so soft and cosy – perfect tiny warmers for perfect newborn hands. They are quick and easy to knit in an evening and make luxurious gifts.

materials

1 50g/1¾oz ball of Jaeger *Cashmina* in either (pale pink/Tea Rose 040), (pale green/Verdigris 042) or (pale blue/Sky 043)

Pair each of 3mm(US 2–3) and 3¼mm(US 3) knitting needles

size

to fit

0–3 mths

tension/gauge

28 sts and 38 rows to 10cm/4in over st-st using 3¼mm(US 3) needles

abbreviations

beg begin(ning); **cm** centimetre(s); **in** inch(es); **k** knit; **k2tog** knit next 2 sts together; **mm** millimetre(s); **p** purl; **rem** remain(ing); **rep** repeat; **RS** right side; **skpo** sl1, k1, psso; **s1** slip next stitch; **st(s)** stitch(es); **st-st** stocking/stockinette stitch; **WS** wrong side

to make (make 2)

With 3mm(US 2–3) needles, cast on 31 sts.
1st row (RS) K1, *p1, k1, rep from * to end.
2nd row (WS) P1, *k1, p1 from * to end.
Rep these 2 rows for 3cm/1¼in, ending with a 2nd row.
Change to 3¼mm(US 3) needles and beg with a k row, work 16 rows in st-st.
shape top
Next row (RS) K1, skpo, k10, k2tog, k1, skpo, k10, k2tog, k1. 27 sts.
Work 3 rows in st-st without shaping.
Next row (RS) K1, skpo, k8, k2tog, k1, skpo, k8, k2tog, k1. 23 sts.
Next row P.
Next row K1, skpo, k6, k2tog, k1, skpo, k6, k2tog, k1. 19 sts.
Next row P.
Cast/bind off.

to finish

Join seam.
Make a 71cm/28in plaited braid and sew one end to inside of each mitten on seam.

cashmere bootees

These little bootees make a great gift for precious new arrivals. Lovely in any colour combination, they feel gloriously luxurious in soft cashmere yarn.

materials

1 50g/1¾oz ball of Jaeger *Cashmina* in each of main colour **M** (dark pink/Cyclamen 047) and **A** (pale pink/Tea Rose 040) or **M** (grey/Pewter 045) and **A** (ecru/Ecru 030)
Pair of 3mm(US 2–3) knitting needles

size

to fit
6–9mths

tension/gauge

28 sts and 38 rows to 10cm/4in over st-st using 3mm(US 2–3) needles

abbreviations

cm centimetre(s); **foll(s)** follow(s)(ing); **g-st (garter stitch)** every row knit; **in** inch(es); **k** knit; **k2tog** knit next 2 sts together; **mm** millimetre(s); **p** purl; **patt** pattern; **rep** repeat; **RS** right side; **st(s)** stitch(es); **st-st** stocking/stockinette stitch; **yo (yarn over needle)** take yarn over right needle to make a st

to make (make 2)

With 3mm(US 2–3) needles and M cast on 41 sts and work 2cm/¾in in g-st.
Change to st-st and work 4 rows.
5th row K2*yo, k2tog,k2, rep from * 8 times, yo, k2tog, k1.
6th row P.
divide for top of foot
7th row K28, turn, p15, turn.
On 15 sts, work stripe patt as folls:
1st row (RS) K in A.
2nd row P in A.
3rd row K in M.
4th row P in M.
5th–20th rows Rep 1st–4th rows 4 times.
21st–22nd rows Rep 1st and 2nd rows once (toe). Break yarns.
With RS facing (13 sts on right needle), rejoin M and pick up and k 16 sts along side of foot, k 15 sts from toe, k 16 sts along side of foot and k 13 sts on left needle. 73 sts.
Work 13 rows in g-st.
shape sole
1st row K1, *k2tog, k30, k2tog* k3, then rep * to * again, k1. 69 sts.
2nd row K31, k2tog, k3, k2tog, k31. 67 sts.
3rd row K1, *k2tog, k27, k2tog* k3, then rep * to * again, k1. 63 sts.
4th row K28, k2tog, k3, k2tog, k28. 61 sts.
5th row K1, *k2tog, k24, k2tog* k3, then rep * to * again, k1. 57 sts.
Cast/bind off.

to finish

Join leg seam and under foot seam. Weave in any loose ends and plait 3 lengths of A together to make ties 43cm/17in long, knotting ends to secure them. Thread ties through eyelets and tie in a bow.

starlight blanket

Sleep under the stars in this snuggly cotton chenille baby blanket. The cosy yarn makes this a great blanket for newborns and those with delicate skins.

materials

8 50g/1¾oz balls of Rowan *Handknit DK Cotton* in main colour **M** (pale blue/Icewater 239) and 2 balls in **A** (dark blue/Galaxy 308)

1 50g/1¾oz balls of Rowan *Chunky Cotton Chenille* in **B** (ecru/Ecru 365)

Pair each 3¾mm(US 5) and 4mm (US 6) knitting needles

2 safety pins

size

Approximately 81x 76cm/32 x 30in

tension/gauge

20 sts and 28 rows to 10cm/4in over st-st using 4mm(US 6) needles

abbreviations

cm centimetre(s); **in** inch(es); **k** knit; **mm** millimetre(s); **p** purl; **rep** repeat; **st(s)** stitch(es); **st-st** stocking/stockinette stitch

note

When working from chart, use separate small balls of yarn for each colour area and twist yarns at colour change to avoid holes.

to make

With 3¾mm(US 5) needles and A, cast on 150 sts and work 7 rows in moss/seed st.

1st row *K1, p1, rep from * to end.

2nd row *P1, k1, rep from * to end.

Work 5 more rows in moss/seed st as established.

8th row Place 5 sts on safety pin, with 4mm(US 6) needles and M, k 140 sts from 1st row of chart, place last 5 sts on safety pin.

On 140 sts, work 2nd–210th rows from chart using intarsia method and st-st, starting with a p row. Leave sts on needle.

edging

With 3¾mm(US 5) needles and A, rejoin yarn to one set of 5 sts on safety pin.

Work in moss/seed st until band fits side of blanket. Rep for other side.

Next row With RS facing and 3¾mm(US 5) needles and A, moss/seed 5 sts from band, k across 140 sts of blanket, moss/seed 5 sts from other band. 150 sts.

Work 7 rows in moss/seed st.

Cast/bind off.

to finish

Weave in any loose ends. Sew edgings to blanket sides.

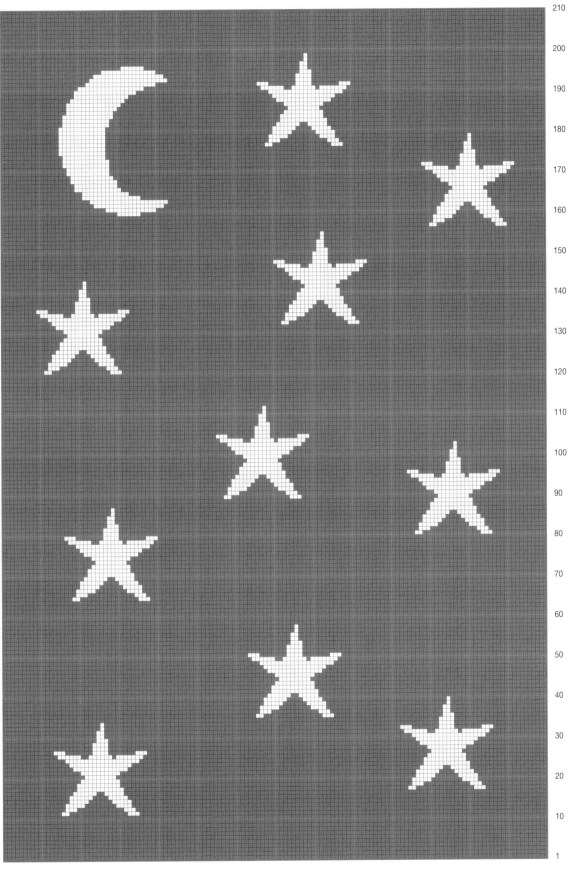

210
200
190
180
170
160
150
140
130
120
110
100
90
80
70
60
50
40
30
20
10
1

moon and stars motif

key

■ M
□ B

floating clouds cushion

Ideal for the nursery, this soft, woolly cloud cushion will be a favourite with all little daydreamers. The pretty buttoned fastening on the back makes it easy to clean, too.

materials

4 50g/1¾oz balls of Rowan *Kid Classic* in main colour **M** (blue/Merry 818) and 2 balls in **A** (ecru/Feather 828)
Pair of 5½mm(US 9) knitting needles
4 buttons
36 x 36cm/14½ x 14½in cushion pad

size

36 x 36cm/14½ x 14½in

tension/gauge

19 sts x 25 rows to 10cm/4in over st-st using 5½mm(US 9) needles

abbreviations

cm centimetre(s); **cont** continue; **in** inch(es); **k** knit; **mm** millimetre(s); **PM** place marker; **p** purl; **rep** repeat; **RS** right side; **st(s)** stitch(es); **st-st** stocking/stockinette stitch

note

When working from chart, use separate small balls of yarn for each colour area and twist yarns at colour change to avoid holes.

to make

Starting with the overlap, with 5½mm(US 9) needles and M, cast on 67 sts.

Work in moss/seed st as follows:

1st–2nd rows *K1, p1, rep from * to last st, k1.

3rd row (buttonhole row) Moss/seed 4 sts, *cast/bind off 2 sts, moss/seed 17 sts, rep from * twice more, cast/bind off 2 sts, moss/seed 4 sts.

4th row Moss/seed 4 sts, *cast on 2 sts, moss/seed 17 sts, rep from * twice more, cast on 2 sts, moss/seed 4 sts.

5th–6th rows Moss/seed st.

Change to st-st and work 45 rows, PM at each end of 39th row for foldline.

46th–166th rows Cont in st-st and using intarsia technique, work from chart, PM at each end of 124th row for foldline. Work 10 rows st st.

Work 14 rows in moss/seed st.

Cast/bind off.

to finish

Weave in loose ends. Fold at markers, RS together, making sure that at the overlap the buttonholes are in the middle of the 'sandwich'. Sew the side seams. Turn RS out. Sew on buttons. Insert cushion pad.

clouds motif

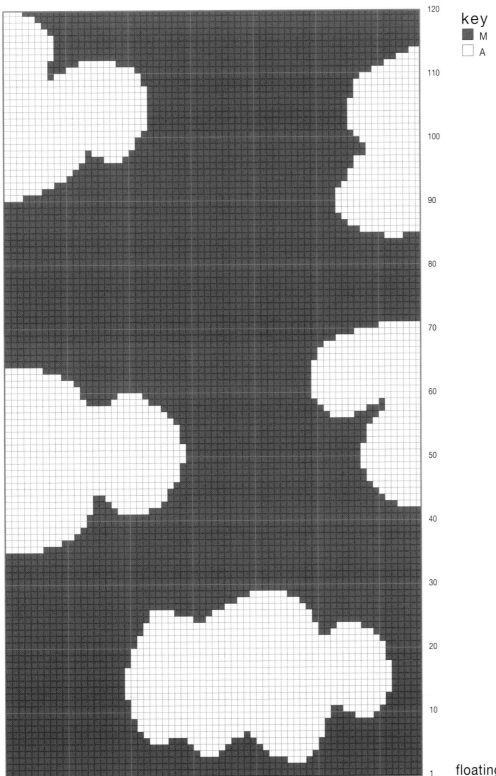

key
M (filled square)
A (white square)

120
110
100
90
80
70
60
50
40
30
20
10
1

kaleidoscope throw

This design was inspired by memories of looking through a kaleidoscope as a child. The bold colours and retro feel will brighten any nursery and stimulate childrens' minds.

materials

5 50/1¾oz balls of Jaeger *Aqua Cotton* in main colour **M** (dark pink/India 322) and 4 balls in each of **A** (red/Ruby 316), **B** (orange/Marigold 331), **C** (yellow/Daffodil 330), **D** (purple/Comfrey 328), **E** (green/Herb 303) and **F** (blue/Blue Agate 317)
Pair each of 4mm(US 6) and 3¼mm(US 3) knitting needles

size

Approximately 94 x 94cm/37 x 37in
Each square 12.5 x 12.5cm/5 x 5in

tension/gauge

22 sts and 30 rows to 10cm/4in over st-st using 4mm(US 6) needles

abbreviations

alt alternate; **cm** centimetre(s); **foll(s)** follow(s)(ing); **in** inch(es); **k** knit; **mm** millimetre(s); **p** purl; **rep** repeat; **st(s)** stitch(es); **st-st** stocking/stockinette stitch

note

When working from chart, substitute different colours for colourways 2–7. Use separate small balls of yarn for each colour area and twist yarns at colour change to avoid holes.

basic square

With 4mm(US 6) needles and M, cast on 28 sts and work 38 rows in st-st foll chart.
Cast/bind off.
make 7 squares in each of the 7 colourways.
Colourway 1 E, F, D, M, A, B.
Colourway 2 A, M, E, C, D, F.
Colourway 3 E, M, B, C, F, A.
Colourway 4 C, B, D, F, E, D.
Colourway 5 B, C, E, D, A, M.
Colourway 6 F, D, A, M, C, E.
Colourway 7 D, E, B, A, M, F.
centre section
To make centre section, stitch squares together in rows of 7, turning alternate squares 180 degrees. Make 4 rows (Rows 1, 3, 5 and 7) with the first square diagonal slanting to the right and 3 rows (Rows 2, 4 and 6) with the first diagonal slanting to the left. Join the rows together to make diamonds, see photograph.

edging

With 3¼mm(US 3) needles and M, cast on 195 sts.
1st–7th rows K1, p1, rep to last st, k1.
8th row Moss/seed 5 sts, cast/bind off 185 sts, moss/seed 5 sts.
On each set of 5 sts, work in moss/seed st until band fits side of blanket.
Next row Moss/seed 5 (band 1), cast on 185 sts, moss/seed 5 (band 2)
Work 7 rows in moss/seed st.
Cast/bind off.

to finish

Weave in loose ends. Stitch edging around centre section.

colourway 1 chart

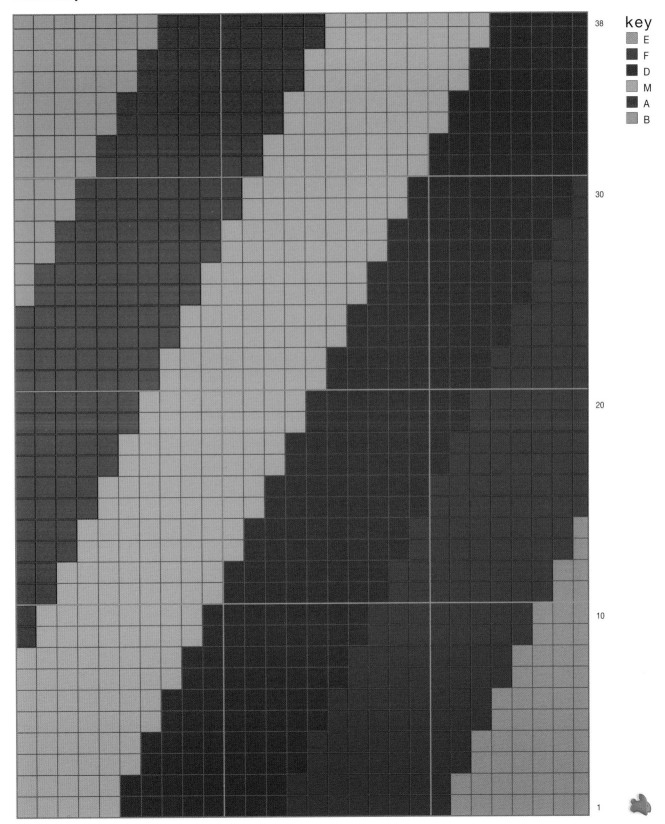

key
- E
- F
- D
- M
- A
- B

30

20

10

1

rainbow cushion

This colourful cushion will brighten up any nursery or bedroom and complements the Kaleidoscope Throw (see page 48).

materials

2 50g/1¾oz balls of Jaeger *Aqua Cotton* in main colour **M** (dark pink/India 322) and small amounts in each of **A** (red/Ruby 316), **B** (orange/Marigold 331), **C** (yellow/Daffodil 330), **D** (purple/Comfrey 328), **E** (green/Herb 303) and **F** (blue/Blue Agate 317)
Pair each of of 4mm(US 6) and 3¾mm(US 5) knitting needles
3 buttons
30 x 30cm/12 x 12in cushion pad

Size

30 x 30cm/12 x 12in

tension/gauge

22 sts and 30 rows to 10 cm/4in over st-st using 4mm(US 6) needles

abbreviations

cm centimetre(s); **in** inch(es); **k** knit; **k2tog** knit next 2 sts together; **mm** millimetre(s); **p** purl; **rep** repeat; **RS** right side; **st(s)** stitch(es); **st-st** stocking/stockinette stitch; **yo (yarn over needle)** take yarn over right needle to make a st

note

When working from chart, use separate small balls of yarn for each colour area and twist yarns at colour change to avoid holes.

to make

With 3¾mm(US 5) needles and M, cast on 66 sts
1st row *K1, p1, rep from * to end.
2nd row *P1, k1, rep from * to end.
Work 20cm/8in in moss/seed st.
Change to 4mm(US 6) needles and work 8 rows in moss/seed st.
9th row Moss/seed 5M, k 1st row of chart, moss/seed 5M.
10th row Moss/seed 5M, p 2nd row of chart, moss/seed 5M.
Cont to complete the 76-row colour chart in st-st while at the same time maintaining the moss/seed st borders in M.
Next row With M, moss/seed 5, k56, moss/seed 5.
Work 7 rows in moss/seed.
Change to 3¾mm(US 5) needles and work 19cm/7½in in moss/seed st.
Next row (buttonhole row) Moss/seed 16 (yo, k2tog, moss/seed 14) 3 times, moss/seed 2.
Work 3 more rows in moss/seed st.
Cast/bind off.

to finish

Fold cushion to make 30 x 30cm/12 x 12in front (RS facing) and sew side seams. (Note that the button holes are in correct position before sewing side seams.) This will give you a 10cm/4in overlap at centre back. Sew on buttons. Insert cushion pad.

rainbow cushion chart

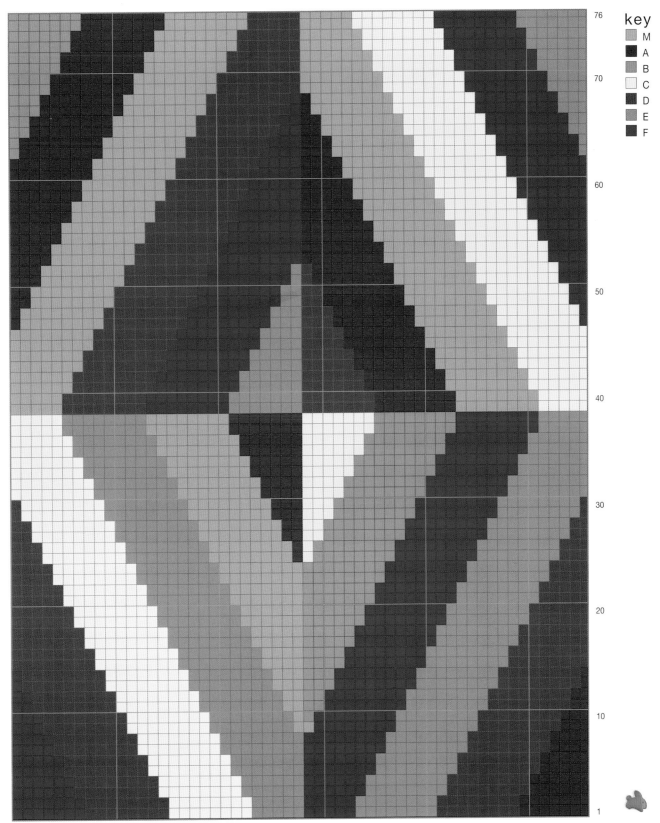

key
- M
- A
- B
- C
- D
- E
- F

 nursery comforts

my first teddy

This woolly bear with his stripy scarf and smiley face is just the sort of bear to become a treasured heirloom. Why not knit a few and have your own teddy bears' picnic?

materials

Teddy: 2 50g/1¾oz balls of Rowan *Cork* in main colour **M** (brown/ Mouse 042)

Scarf: 1 50g/1¾oz ball of Rowan 4 ply *Soft* in each of **A** (red/Honk 374) and **B** (ecru/Nippy 376)

Pair each of 3mm(US 2–3) and 4½mm(US 7) knitting needles

2 safety pins

Washable stuffing

Black or brown yarn for eyes and nose embroidery

size

41cm/16in tall

tension/gauge

Teddy: 12 sts and 18 rows to 10cm/ 4in over st-st using 4½mm(US 7) needles

Scarf: 28 sts and 36 rows to 10cm/ 4in over st-st using 3mm(US 2–3) needles

abbreviations

alt alternate; **cm** centimetre(s); **cont** continue; **dec** decreas(e)(ing); **foll(s)** follow(s)(ing); **inc** increas(e)(ing); **in** inch(es); **inc** increase in next stitch; **k** knit; **k2tog** knit next 2 sts together; **m1** make 1 st by picking up and working into back of loop lying between last st and next st; **mm** millimetre(s); **p** purl; **p2tog** purl next 2 sts together; **patt** pattern; **psso** pass slipped st over; **rem** remain(ing); **rep** repeat; **RS** right side; **s1** slip next st; **skpo** s1, k1, psso; **st(s)** stitch(es); **st-st** stocking/stockinette stitch; **tbl** through back of loop; **WS** wrong side

1st row K7, cast/bind off 10 sts, k14, cast/bind off 10 sts, k3, place last 4 sts on safety pin.

work head

WS facing, p3, p14, p3, place last 4 sts on safety pin. 20 sts on needle.

shape face

1st row K10, m1, k10. 21 sts.

2nd row Inc in 1st st, p to last 2 sts, inc in next st, p1. 23 sts.

3rd row K11, m1, k1, m1, k11. 25 sts.

4th row As 2nd row. 26 sts.

5th row K13, m1, k1, m1, k13. 29 sts.

6th row As 2nd row. 31 sts.

7th row K15, m1, k1, m1, k15. 33 sts.

8th row As 2nd row. 35 sts.

9th row K17, m1, k1, m1, k17. 37 sts.

10th row As 2nd row. 39 sts.

11th row K19, m1, k1, m1, k19. 41 sts.

Work 2 rows in st-st.

14th row P20, cast/bind off 1 st, p20.

15th row On 20 sts, k18, k2tog. 19 sts.

16th row P2tog, p17. 18 sts.

17th row K16, k2tog. 17 sts.

18th row P.

19th row Skpo, k13, k2tog. 15 sts.

20th row P.

21st row Skpo, k11, k2tog. 13 sts.

22nd row P2tog, p9, p2tog. 11 sts.

23rd row Cast/bind off 3 sts, k to end. 8 sts.

24th row Cast/bind off 3 sts, p to end. 5 sts.

Cast/bind off.

With RS facing rejoin yarn to rem 20 sts and work from 15th row to end, reversing all shapings.

shape top of head

Sew small shoulder seams and centre back body seam. Place sts on safety pins back onto needle. 8 sts. With RS facing, rejoin yarn and work as follows:

1st row K.

2nd row Inc in 1st st, p to last 2 sts, inc in next st, p1. 10 sts.

3rd–10th rows Rep 1st–2nd rows 4 times. 18 sts.

11th–20th rows Work in st-st without shaping.

21st row K2tog, k to last 2 sts, skpo. 16 sts.

22nd–30th rows Work in st-st without shaping.

body

With 4½mm(US 7) needles and M, cast on 40 sts.

1st row *K2, inc in next st, k2, rep from * to end. 48 sts.

Starting with a p row, cont in st-st until work measures 12.5cm/5in, ending with a p row.

31st row K2tog, k to last 2 sts, skpo. 14 sts.
32nd–36th rows Work in st-st without shaping.
37th row K2tog, k to last 2 sts, skpo. 12 sts.
38th row P.
39th row K2tog, k to last 2 sts, skpo. 10 sts.
40th row P.
41st and 43rd rows K2tog, k to last 2 sts, skpo.
42nd and 44th rows P2tog tbl, k to last 2 sts, skpo.
2 sts.
45th row K2tog. Fasten off.
Carefully ease top of head piece around face and sew.
Stuff head and body. Sew lower body seam.

legs

With 4½mm(US 7) needles and M, cast on 12 sts.
1st row *K1, inc in next st, rep from * to end. 18 sts.
2nd row P.
3rd row Inc in 1st st, k6, inc in next st, k2, inc in
next st, k6, inc in next st. 22 sts.
4th row P.
5th row K8, inc in next st, k3, inc in next st, k9. 24
sts
6th–10th rows Work in st-st without shaping.
11th row K10, skpo, k2tog, k10. 22 sts.
12th row P.
13th row K9, skpo, k2tog, k9. 20 sts.
Work 31 rows in st-st without shaping.
Cast/bind off.
Make second leg to match.
RS facing, join foot and leg seam, leaving cast/bind-off
edge open. Turn RS out and stuff. Make seam centre
back of leg and close opening. Attach legs to body.

arms

left arm
With 4½mm(US 7) needles and M, cast on 16 sts.
1st row *Inc in 1st st, k6 [inc in next st] twice, k6, inc
in next st. 20 sts.
Work 23 rows in st-st, starting with a p row. #
work paw
25th row K3, p1, k1, p1, k14.
26th row P13, *k1, p1, rep from * once, k1, p2.

27th–32nd row Rep 25th–26th rows 3 times.
33rd row As 25th row.
34th row *P2tog, p6, p2tog, rep from * once. 16 sts.
35th row K.
36th row *P1, p2tog, rep from * to last stitch, p1.
Cast/bind off.
right arm
Work as for Left Arm from # to #.
work paw
25th row K14, p1, k1, p1, k3.
26th row P2, *k1, p1, rep from * once, k1, p13.
Cont and finish as for Left Arm, noting paw position.
RS facing, join arm seam, leaving cast/bind-off edge
open. Turn RS out and stuff. Close opening. Attach to
body with seams on the underside of the arm.

ears (make 2)

With 4½mm(US 7) needles and M, cast on 10 sts.
Work 3 rows in st-st.
Dec 1 st at each end of next and foll alt row. 6 sts.
Work 1 row in st-st without shaping.
8th row *K1, p1, rep from * to end.
9th row Inc in 1st st, *k1 p1, rep from * once, inc in
next st. 8 sts.
10th–14th row Work in moss/seed st.
Cast/bind off in moss/seed st.
Make second ear to match.
Fold ear in half and sew side seams. Attach to head
with moss/seed st as front of ear.

to finish

Weave in loose ends. Embroider eyes, mouth and nose.

scarf

With 3mm(US 2–3) needles and A, cast on 15 sts.
Work approximately 50cm/20in in moss/seed st with
stripe patt of *4 rows A, 4 rows B*, ending with 4
rows A.
Cast/bind off.
Weave in loose ends. Tie scarf around Teddy's neck.

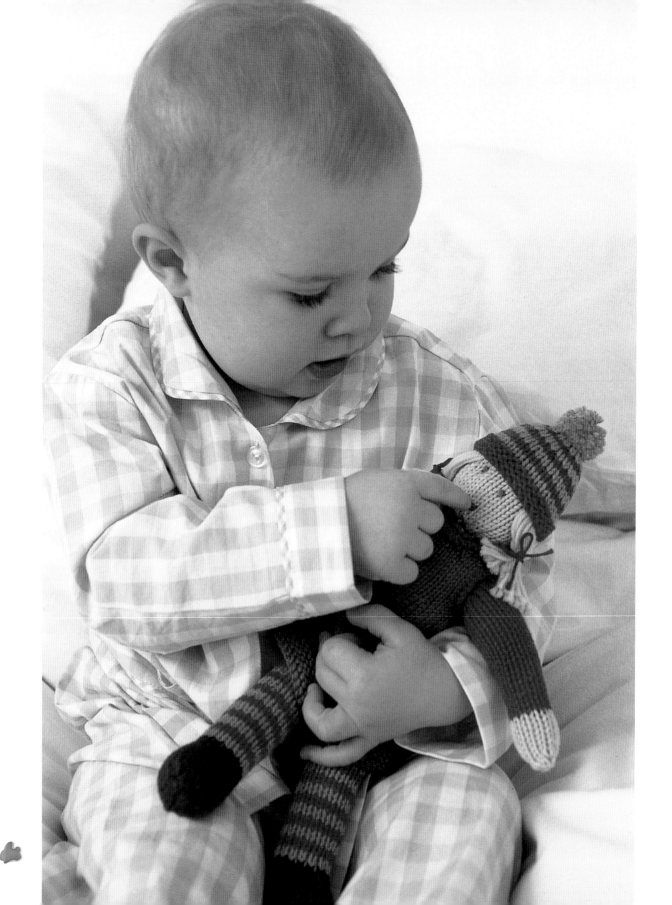

darling dolly

This dolly is a firm favourite with my little one and is a good way to use up oddments of yarn. Try knitting several different dollies, then they can all play together.

materials

Oddments of Jaeger *Aqua Cotton* in (orange/Marigold 331), (dark pink/India 322), (flesh colour/Talc 302), (yellow/Daffodil 330), (red/Ruby 316) and (purple/Comfrey328)

Pair of 3mm(US 2–3) knitting needles

Crochet hook

Washable stuffing

size

31cm/12½in tall

tension/gauge

26 sts and 36 rows to 10cm/4in over st-st using 3mm(US 2–3) needles

abbreviations

alt alternate; **beg** begin(ning); **cm** centimetre(s); **cont** continue; **in** inch(es); **inc** increas(e)(ing); **k** knit; **k2tog** knit next 2 sts together; **mm** millimetre(s); **p** purl; **p2tog** purl next 2 sts together; **patt** pattern; **psso** pass slipped st over; **rem** remain(ing); **rep** repeat; **RS** right side; **s1** slip next st; **skpo** s1, k1, psso; **st(s)** stitch(es); **st-st** stocking/stockinette stitch; **WS** wrong side

note

Work in st-st throughout unless specified otherwise.

body

With 3mm(US 2–3) needles and body colour, cast on 24 sts and work 2 rows in st-st marking the 12th and 13th sts.

3rd row *K2, inc in next st, rep from * to end. 32 sts. Work 25 rows st-st without shaping beg with p row.

shape shoulders

1st row K6, skpo, k2tog, k12, skpo, k2tog, k6. 28 sts.
2nd and 4th rows P.
3rd row K5, skpo, k2tog, k10, skpo, k2tog, k5. 24 sts.
5th row K4, skpo, k2tog, k8, skpo, k2tog, k4. 20 sts.
6th row K.
7th row Change to flesh colour. Work 2 rows in st-st beg with a k row.

shape head

1st row *K1, inc in next st, rep from * to end. 30 sts. Work 21 rows in st-st beg with a p row.

shape top of head

1st row *K3, k2tog*, rep from * to end. 24 sts.
2nd and 4th rows P.
3rd row *K3, k2tog, rep from * to end. 18 sts.
5th row *K1, k2tog, rep from * to end. 12 sts.
6th row *P2tog, rep from * to end. 6 sts.
Break yarn leaving 25cm/10in end. Thread yarn through remaining 6 stitches and pull up tightly. Fasten securely. Join head seam and body seam (row ends), leaving an opening for stuffing. Place seam between markers on cast-on edge and oversew across cast-on edge, making

the seam centre back. Turn RS out and stuff firmly. Close opening. Embroider eyes, nose and mouth.

legs (make 2)

With 3mm(US 2–3) needles and shoe colour, cast on 14 sts.

1st row *K1, inc in next st, rep from * to end. 21 sts.
2nd row P.
3rd row K7, *inc in next st, k1 rep from * 3 times, k6. 25 sts.
4th–10th rows Work in st-st without shaping, beg with a p row.
11th row K7, [skpo] twice, s1, k2tog, psso, [k2tog] twice, k7. 19 sts.
12th row P.
13th row K2tog, k15, k2tog. 17 sts.
Change to stocking colours and work 36 rows in st-st in 2-row stripes, starting with a p row.
49th row P1, p2tog, p3, p2tog, p1, p2tog, p3, p2tog, p1. 13 sts.
Cast/bind off.
Join stocking and shoe seams leaving cast/bind-off edge open. Turn RS out and stuff. Make stocking seam centre back of leg and close opening. Attach legs to body.

arms (make 2)

With 3mm(US 2–3) needles and flesh colour, cast on 4 sts.

1st row Inc in each stitch. 8 sts.
2nd row P.
3rd row Inc in 1st st, k2, [inc in next st] twice, k2, inc in next st.
4th row Inc in 1st st, p9, inc in next st, p1. 14 sts. Work 6 rows in st-st without shaping, beg with a knit row.
Change to dark pink and work 25 rows in st-st, inc 1 st at each end of row 11. 16 sts.
Next row *P2, p2tog, rep from * to end. 12 sts.
Cast/bind off.
Join arm seam, leaving cast/bind-off edge open. Turn RS out and stuff. Close opening. Attach to body,

having the seams on the underside of the arm and the top of the arm at the second shoulder decrease.

dress

With 3 mm(US 2–3) needles and dress colour, cast on 60 sts and k5 rows.

Change to st-st and work 32 rows, beg with a k row, decreasing on rows 11, 21 and 31 rows as follows:

11th row K3, *skpo, k8, skpo, k2tog, k8, k2tog* k6, rep * to * once, k3. 52 sts.

21st row K3, *skpo, k6, skpo, k2tog, k6, k2tog*, k6, rep from * to * once, k3. 44 sts.

31st row K3, *skpo, k4, skpo, k2tog, k4, k2tog*, k6, rep from * to * once, k3. 36 sts.

shape armholes

33rd row K8, cast/bind off 2 sts, k16, cast/bind off 2 sts, k8.

On 8 sts, work Right Back.

1st row P6, p2tog. 7 sts.

2nd–8th rows Work in st-st.

shape neck

9th row Cast/bind off 3 sts, p to end. 4 sts.

10th row K.

11th row P2tog, p2. 3 sts.

12th row K.

13th row P.

Cast/bind off.

On 16 sts, work front.

1st row WS facing, rejoin yarn, p2tog, p12, p2tog. 14 sts.

Work 6 rows in st-st.

shape neck

8th row K5, cast/bind off 4 sts, k5.

**Dec 1 st at neck edge on next and foll alt row.

Work 2 rows.

Cast/bind off**.

Rejoin yarn to right front neck and work from ** to ** to match.

left back

WS facing, rejoin yarn to rem 8 sts and work to match Right Back.

edgings

arm trims (both alike)

With RS facing and with 3mm(US 2–3) needles and a contrast colour, pick up 24 sts around armhole.

Cast/bind off knitwise.

Join shoulder seams.

neck trim

With RS facing and with 3mm(US 2–3) needles and a contrasting colour, pick up 30 sts around neck.

Cast/bind off knitwise.

to finish

Join centre back seam from hem to armhole. **Do not break thread**. Fit dress onto doll and complete centre back seam.

hat

With 3mm(US 2–3) needles and one of the colours used for the stockings, cast on 32 sts and k 5 rows.

Change to other stocking colour and work 8 rows in 2-row stripes, starting with a knit row.

shape top

1st row *K2 k2tog, rep from * to end. 24 sts.

Work 3 rows st-st.

5th row *K1, k2tog, rep from * to end. 16 sts.

Work 3 rows st-st.

9th row *K2tog, rep from * to end. 8 sts.

10th row *P2tog, rep from * to end. 4 sts.

Finish off as for top of head. Sew side seam. Buy (or make) small pompon and attach to top of hat.

hair

Cut long strands of yarn, fold in half and knot through knitted stitches on head using a crochet hook. Part strands along centre of head to form two bunches and tie with lengths of contrasting yarn. Trim strands to neaten.

playful penguin

This fun penguin with its bright orange beak and feet is great for newborns as well as toddlers. Its monotone colour scheme is also said to stimulate babies.

materials

1 50g/1¾oz ball of Jaeger *Matchmaker Merino DK* in main colour **M** (black/Black 681) and small amounts in **A** (cream/Cream 622) and **B** (orange/Pumpkin 898).
Oddment of yellow yarn for eyes
Pair of 3mm(US 2–3) knitting needles
Washable stuffing

size

20cm/8in tall

tension/gauge

28 sts and 38 rows to 10cm/4in over st-st using 3mm(US 2–3) needles

abbreviations

beg begin(ning); **cm** centimetre(s); **cont** continue; **dec** decreas(e)(ing); **foll(s)** follow(s)(ing); **inc** increas(e)(ing); **in** inch(es); **k** knit; **k2tog** knit next 2 sts together; **mm** millimetre(s); **p** purl; **p2tog** purl next 2 sts together; **rem** remain(ing); **st(s)** stitch(es); **st-st** stocking/stockinette stitch; **tbl** through back of loops

base

With 3mm (US 2–3) needles and M, cast on 28 sts.
Work 19 rows in st-st, dec 1 st at each end of 5th, 9th, 13th, 17th and 19th rows. 18 sts.
Work 1 row.
Dec 1 st at each end of next 4 rows. 10 sts.
Cast/bind off 3 sts at beg next 2 rows. 4 sts.
Cast/bind off.

body

With 3mm (US 2–3) needles and M, cast on 79 sts.
Work 6 rows in st-st, inc 1 st at each end of 3rd and 6th rows. 83 sts.
7th row K39M, k5A, k39M.
8th row P37M, p9A, p37M.
9th row Inc in 1st st, k35M, k11A, k35M, inc in last st. 85 sts.
10th row P36M, p13A, p36M.
11th row K36M, k13A, k36M.
12th row P35M, p15A, p35M.
13th row K2tog, k33M, k15A, k33M, k2tog tbl. 83 sts.
14th row P2tog tbl, p32M, p15A, p32M, p2tog, 81 sts.
15th row K2tog, k31M, k15A, k31M, k2tog tbl. 79 sts.
16th row P32M, p15A, p32M.
17th row K2tog, k30M, k15A, k30M, k2tog tbl. 77 sts.
18th row P31M, p15A, p31M.
19th row K31M, k15A, k31M.
20th row P2tog tbl, p21M, p2tog tbl, p6M, p15A, p6M, p2tog, p21M, p2tog. 73 sts.
21st, 23rd, 25th and 27th rows K29M, k15A, k29M.
22nd, 24th, 26th and 28th rows P29M, p15A, p29M.
29th row K2tog, k20M, k2tog, k5M, k15A, k5M, k2tog tbl, k20M, k2tog tbl. 69 sts.
30th row P27M, p15A, p27M.
31st row K27M, k15A, k27M.
32nd and 34th rows P28M, p13A, p28M.
33rd row K28M, k13A, k28M.
35th row K2tog. k19M, k2tog, k5M, k13A, k5M,

k2tog tbl, k19M, k2tog tbl. 65 sts.
36th row P26M, p13A, p26M.
37th row K26M, k13A, k26M.
38th row P27M, p11A, p27M.
39th row K27M, k11A, k27M.
40th row P28M, p9A, p28M.
41st row K7M, k2tog, k14M, k2tog, k5M, k5A, k5M, k2tog tbl, k14M, k2tog tbl, k7M. 61 sts.
Break A.
42nd–46th rows Work in st-st using M only.
Cont in st-st using M to 70th row, shaping as follows (shaping rows ONLY given from this point).
47th row K6, k2tog, k14, k2tog, k13, k2tog, k14, k2tog, k6. 57 sts.
53rd row K6, k2tog, k12, k2tog, k13, k2tog, k12, k2tog, k6. 53 sts.
59th row K5, k2tog, k12, k2tog, k11, k2tog, k12, k2tog, k6. 49 sts.
65th row *K4, k2tog, rep from * to last st, k1. 41 sts.
66th row P1, *p2tog, p3, rep from * to end. 33 sts.
67th row *K2tog, k2, rep from * to last st, k1. 25 sts.
68th row P1, *p2tog, p1, rep from * to end. 17 sts.
69th row *K2tog, rep from * to last st, k1. 9 sts.
70th row P1, *p2tog, rep from * to end. 5 sts.
Break yarn and thread through rem sts, draw tightly and fasten off securely.

wings (both alike)
With 3mm(US 2–3) needles and M, cast on 6 sts and knit 1 row.
Cont in st-st.
Cast on 2 sts beg of next 2 rows. 10 sts.
Work 1 row.
Inc 1 st at each end of next and foll 4th row. 14 sts.
Work 21 rows without shaping.
Dec 1 st at each end of next and foll 4th row. 10 sts.
Work 1 row.
Cast/bind off 2 sts beg next 2 rows. 6 sts.
Cast/bind off.

beak
With 3mm(US 2–3) needles and B, cast on 17 sts and knit 4 rows in st-st.

Cont in st-st, dec 1 st at each end of next 7 rows. 3 sts.
Work 1 row.
Inc 1 st at each end of next 7 rows. 17 sts.
Work 5 rows st-st without shaping.
Cast/bind off.

feet (both alike)
With 3mm(US 2–3) needles and B, cast on 13 sts and work 16 rows in st-st, inc 1 st at each end of 7th and 13th rows. 17 sts.
Cont in st-st to 32nd row, dec 1 st at each end of 21st and 27th rows. 13 sts.
Cast/bind off.

to finish
Fold beak in half widthways and sew side seams. Fold feet in half widthways and sew side seams. Embroider toes with M. Attach feet to cast-on edge of base. Join centre back seam of body from head to halfway down. Insert base with the cast-on edge and feet to front of body and cast/bind-off edge of base to tail side of body. Sew into position, then sew tail and back seam of body, leaving opening for stuffing. Stuff body and close opening. Stuff beak and sew in a rounded shape to face. Embroider eyes with yellow yarn. Fold wings in half lengthways and sew side seams. Attach to body.

zoo toy bag

Handy for trips to grandma's house, this elephant-design toy bag will hold lots of favourite toys. At home, it looks stylish hanging on the nursery door and keeps toys tidy.

materials

3 balls of Rowan *Handknit DK Cotton* in **A** (dark green/Slippery 316), 2 balls in **B** (pale green/Celery 309), 2 balls in **C** (yellow/Zing 300), 2 balls in **D** (ecru/Ecru 251), 2 balls in **E** (beige/Linen 205) and 2 balls in **F** (dark beige/Tope 253)

Pair of 4mm(US 6) knitting needles
Spare knitting needle

size

45 x 53cm/18 x 21in

tension/gauge

20 sts and 28 rows to 10cm/4in over st-st using 4mm(US 6) needles

abbreviations

cm centimetre(s); **foll(s)** follow(s)(ing); **in** inch(es); **k** knit; **mm** millimetre(s); **p** purl; **RS** right side; **st(s)** stitch(es); **st-st** stocking/stockinette stitch

note

Work in st-st throughout. When working from chart, use separate small balls of yarn for each colour area and twist yarns at colour change to avoid holes.

pocket lining

With 4mm(US 6) needles and E, cast on 36 sts and work 40 rows in st-st.
Leave sts on spare needle.

bag

With 4mm(US 6) needles and A, cast on 90 sts and work 20 rows in st-st.
Foll chart working 1st–140th rows in st-st, ignoring elephant pocket.
Turn chart upside down and work 141st–180th rows.
181st row K27E, k36 sts from 1st row of elephant pocket chart, k27E.
182nd row P27E, p36 sts from 2nd row of elephant pocket chart, pp27E.
183rd–220th rows Work in st-st following chart.
221st row With A, k27, *p2, k2, rep from * 8 times, p2, k26.
222nd row P26, *k2, p2, rep from * 8 times, k2, p26.
223rd and 224th rows As 221st and 222nd rows.
225th row K27, cast/bind off 36 sts, k27.
226th row (place pocket) P27, p across 36 sts of pocket lining from spare needle, p27.
227th and 280th rows Work in st-st following chart.
Change to A and work 20 more rows in st-st.
Cast/bind off.

ties (make 2)

With 4mm(US 6) needles and B, cast on 5 sts and work 100cm(40in) in st-st.
Cast/bind off.

to finish

Weave in any loose ends. Slip stitch pocket lining into place. Fold end 20 rows in half and stitch down seams to the inside of the bag to make a casing for the ties. Fold bag in half RS facing and stitch side seams, leaving casing seams open. Thread ties through casing, left to right and right to left (see photograph). Sew the ends of each tie together to make a loop.

zoo toy bag chart

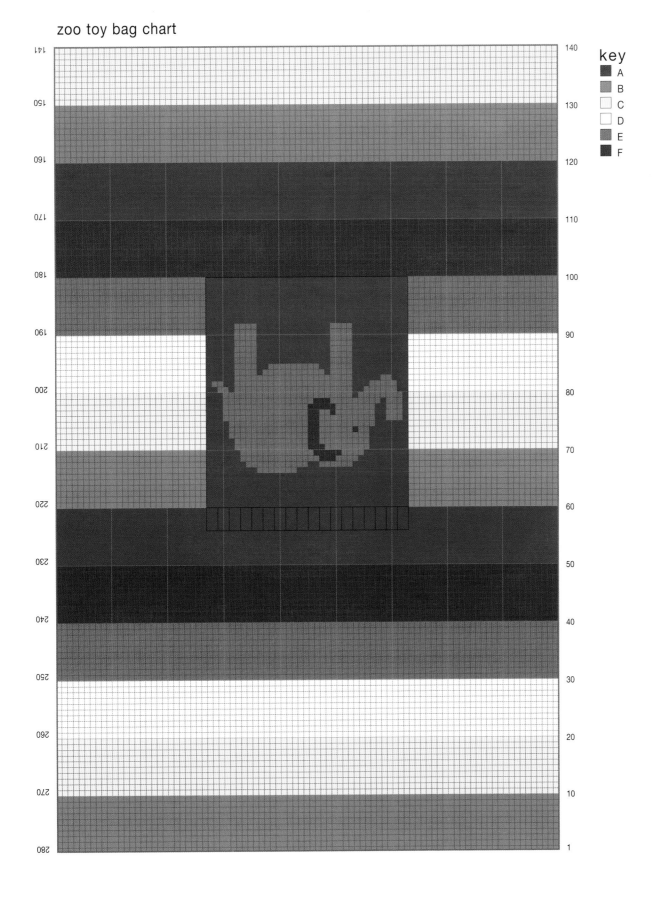

key
A
B
C
D
E
F

play cubes

These cubes are the perfect height for toddlers to sit on and have a useful side pocket for storing books and toys. They are fun and functional and can be stacked to save space.

materials

Green cube: 2 50g/1¾oz balls of Rowan *Handknit DK Cotton* in each of (pale green/Celery 309), (dark green/Slippery 316) and (blue/Galaxy 308)

Pink cube: 2 50g/1¾oz balls of Rowan *Handknit DK Cotton* in each of (pale pink/Sugar 303), (dark pink/Slick 313) and (red/Rosso 215)

Pair of 4mm(US 6) knitting needles
Washable filling

size

Each face of cube 30cm/12in square

tension/gauge

20 sts and 28 rows to 10cm/4in using st-st and 4mm(US 6) needles

abbreviations

cm centimetre(s); **foll(s)** follow(s)(ing); **in** inch(es); **k** knit; **mm** millimetre; **p** purl; **st(s)** stitch(es); **st-st** stocking/stockinette stitch

basic square

With 3mm(US 6) needles, cast on 60 sts and work 84 rows in st-st.

Cast/bind off.

Make 6 squares to make 1 cube.

patch pocket

With 3mm(US 6) needles, cast on 40 sts and work 55 rows in st-st.

56th row *k2, p2, rep from * to end.

Repeat 56th row 6 times more. (7 rows k2, p2 rib in all.)

Cast/bind off in k2, p2 rib.

green cube

Make 2 squares in dark green, 1 square each in light green and blue, 1 square working in stripes of 4 rows light green and 4 rows dark green and 1 square working in stripes of 4 rows blue and 4 rows dark green.

Work patch pocket in light green.

pink cube

Make 2 squares in dark pink, 1 square each in light pink and red, 1 square working in stripes of 4 rows light pink and 4 rows dark pink and 1 square working in stripes of 4 rows dark pink and 4 rows red.

Work patch pocket in red.

to finish

Sew patch pocket to a dark green or dark pink square. Join 6 squares together following the illustration below and leaving one seam open. Stuff cube with filling and close seam.

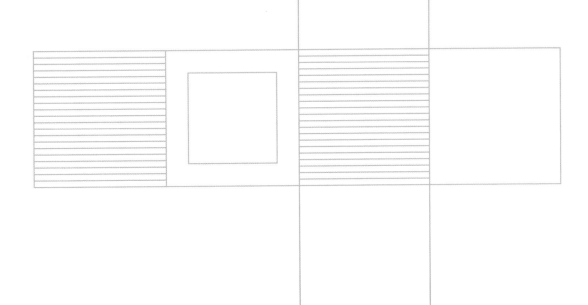

party flags

Perfect for birthday parties and special occasions, these flags are a great way to use up bits of leftover yarns. They are also a fun way to add colour to your child's nursery.

materials

Jaeger *Aqua Cotton* 15g each of two colours per flag: (yellow/Daffodil 330), (orange/Marigold 331), pale pink/Anemone 327), (dark pink/India 322), (red/Ruby 316), (purple/Comfrey 328), (green/Herb 303), (blue/Blue Agate 317), (dark blue/Deep 320)

Pair of 4mm(US 6) knitting needles

Cord, long enough to pass through all the flags and to make hanging loops at each end.

size

Each flag 20cm/8in long

tension/gauge

22 sts and 30 rows to 10cm/4in over st-st using 4mm(US 6) needles

abbreviations

cm centimetre(s); **dec** decreas(e)(ing); **foll(s)** follow(s)(ing); **in** inch(es); **k** knit; **k2tog** knit next 2 sts together; **mm** millimetre(s); **p** purl; **p2tog** purl next 2 sts together; **patt** pattern; **psso** pass slipped st over; **rem** remain(ing); **rep** repeat; **s1** slip next st; **skpo** s1, k1, psso; **st(s)** stitch(es); **st-st** stocking/stockinette stitch; **tbl** through back of loops; **WS** wrong side

notes

Work in st-st throughout, but k the first and last stitch on the p rows. When working from chart, use separate small balls of yarn for each colour area and twist yarns at colour change to avoid holes.

basic flag

With 4mm(US 6) needles, cast on 42 sts and work 10 rows.

11th row K2, skpo, k to last 4 sts, k2tog, k2.
12th–13th rows St-st.
14th row K1, p1, p2tog, p to last 4 sts, p2tog tbl, p1 k1.
15th–16th rows Work in st-st.
Rep 11th–16th rows until 6 sts rem. 64th row.
65th row K1, s1, k2tog, psso, k2.
66th–67th rows Work in st-st.
68th row K2tog, k2tog.
Cast/bind off.

to finish

Make a hem to thread cord through bunting by turning over first 4 rows to WS and stitching to back of flag. Weave in any loose ends.

striped flags

Work first 8 rows in A and then in stripe patt of 4 rows B, 4 rows A, repeating these last 8 rows throughout.
Flag 1 A orange, B dark pink
Flag 2 A green, B mid blue
Flag 3 A purple, B dark pink
Flag 4 A pale pink, B dark pink
Flag 5 A yellow, B green

spotted flags

Foll chart, remembering to work decs on 3rd and 4th stitches from edges.
Flag 1 A red, B orange
Flag 2 A dark pink, B pale pink
Flag 3 A dark blue, B pale blue
Flag 4 A green, B light blue
Flag 5 A orange, B yellow

spotted flag chart

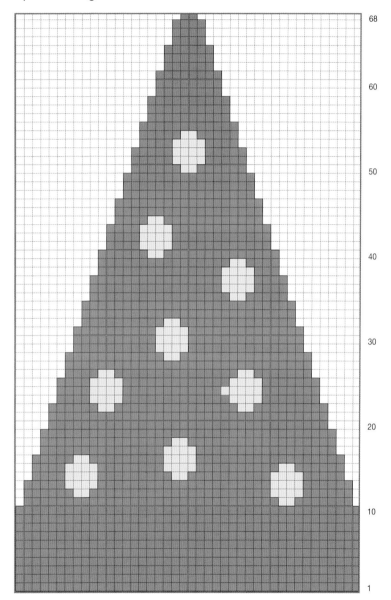

key
A
B

my own puppet theatre

This theatre is sure to keep little ones amused and entertained for hours. It can be hung at various heights for taller or shorter children and is easy to put up.

materials

3 50g/1¾oz balls of Rowan *Handknit DK Cotton* in **A** (yellow/ Sunflower 304), 6 balls in **B** (blue/Galaxy 308), 3 balls in **C** (green/Gooseberry 219), 3 balls in **D** (red/Rosso 215), 1 ball in **E** (orange/Flame 254), and 2 balls in **F** (white/Ecru 251)

Small amounts of Rowan *Handknit DK Cotton* for head, hair and garments.

Oddments of Rowan *Handknit DK Cotton* to embroider eyes, mouth and nose

Pair of 4mm(US 6) knitting needles

Spare knitting needle

5.5m/18 feet tape, 4cm/1½in wide

60cm/24in hook and loop tape, 2cm/¾–1 in wide

1m/3 feet round wooden dowelling with 1.2cm/½in flat edge

size

Theatre: 81cm/32in wide and 137cm/54in long, plus edging

Glove puppets: 21.5cm/8½in tall

tension/gauge

20 sts and 28 rows to 10cm/4in over st-st using 4mm(US 6) needles

abbreviations

beg begin(ning); **cm** centimetre(s); **dec** decreas(e)(ing); **foll** follow(ing); **in** inch(es); **inc** increas(e)(ing); **k** knit; **p** purl; **RS** right side; **st(s)** stitch(es); **st-st** stocking/stockinette stitch; **WS** wrong side

note

When working from chart, use separate small balls of yarn for each colour area and twist yarns at colour change to avoid holes.

Break yarns and leave sts on spare needle.
Work 2nd set of 35 sts to match, foll chart 1. Do **not** break B.

Next row With B, k2, p33, cast on 89 sts, then working from sts on spare needle, p33, k2. 159 sts.

Work 1st–55th rows of chart 2 in st-st, keeping the k2 at the outer edges and working stars using the intarsia technique.

56th row K, to make a foldline.

Work 8 more rows in st-st.

Cast/bind off.

pointed edging

With 4mm(US 6) needles and B, cast 2 sts and work as follows.

1st row K2.

2nd row Inc in 1st st, k1. 3 sts.

3rd row K1, p1 inc in 3rd st. 4 sts.

4th row Inc in 1st st, k1, p1, k1. 5 sts.

5th–8th rows Cont in moss/seed st, inc at shaped edge on every row. 9 sts.

9th row Work in moss/seed st without shaping.

10th–16th rows Work in moss/seed st dec at shaped edge on every row, moss/seed st. 2 sts.

Repeat 1st–16th rows until straight edge fits along bottom of theatre.

Cast/bind off.

to make

With 4mm(US 6) needles and A, cast on 159 sts.

1st–4th rows K2, *p1, k1, rep from * to last 3 sts, p1 k2.

5th row K.

6th row K2, p to last 2 sts, k2.

7th–28th rows Rep 5th–6th rows 11 times.

29th row Change to B. K.

30th row With B, k2, p to last 2 sts, k2.

31st–56th rows Rep 29th–30th rows 13 times.

Cont in 28-row stripes, using C,D,E and then A,B and C until 27th row of the 2nd C stripe.

Next row K2, p31, k2, cast/bind off 89 sts, k2, p31, k2. On first set of 35 sts, work right side of stage.

Work 1st–97th rows of chart 1 in st-st, keeping k2 at the outer edges and working stars using intarsia technique.

curtains (make 2)

With 4mm(US 6) needles and D, cast on 85 sts.

1st–4th rows Work in moss st.

5th row K1, p1, k1, p1, k to last 4 sts, p1, k1, p1, k1.

6th row K1, p1, k1, p1, p to last 4 sts, p1, k1, p1, k1.

7th–8th rows As 5th and 6th rows.

**9th–16th rows Change to F and repeat 5th–6th rows 4 times.

17th–24th rows Change to D and repeat 5th–6th rows 4 times.**

Repeat from ** to ** 3 times, then 9th–16th rows again.

Change to D and work 5th–8th rows, then work 1st–4th rows.

Cast/bind off in moss/seed st.

puppet theatre chart 1

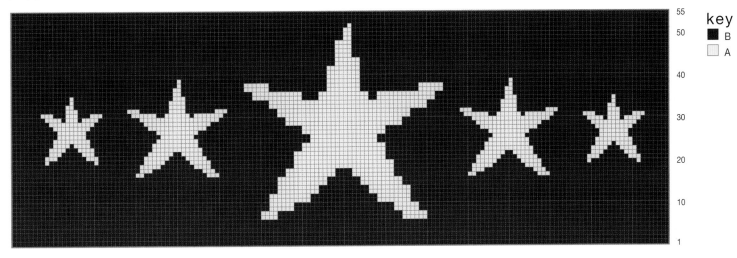

key
■ B
▨ A

puppet theatre chart 2

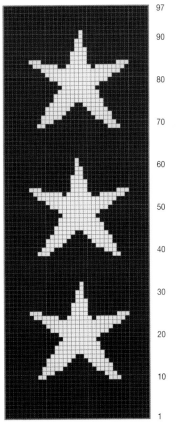

97
90

80

70

60

50

40

30

20

10

1

key
■ B
☐ A

 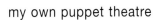

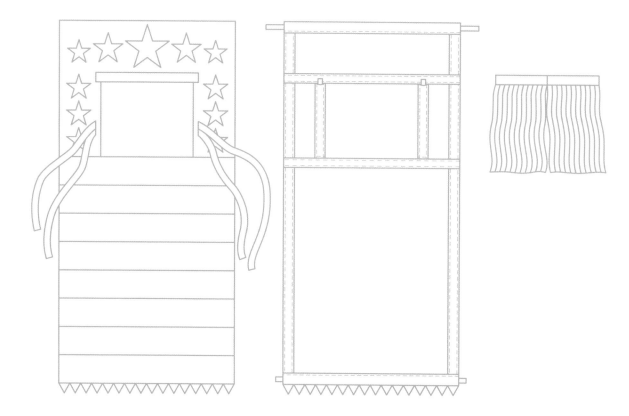

to finish

Weave in any loose ends. Fold top edge to WS at foldline and sew cast/bind off edge to WS of piece to make a casing to take dowelling for hanging. Sew tape across the WS of piece, level with top, bottom and sides of opening for re-enforcing with semi-circular dowelling. On each side of opening, fold a 122cm/48in length of tape in half and sew fold line one-third up on WS. Sew hook and loop tape across top of opening (on RS) and across one WS side edge of each of the curtains (stripes are vertical). Sew straight side of pointed edging to cast-on edge of theatre. Cut dowelling to size and insert into casings.

girl body (back and front alike)

With 4mm(US 6) needles and garment colour, cast on 32 sts and k 3 rows.
Change to contrasting colour and work 2 rows in st-st beg with a k row.
Change to garment colour, k 1 row and cont in st-st beg

with a k row, dec 1 st each end of 1st and every foll 6th row to 22 sts. Cont in st-st until work measures 12cm/4¾in, ending with a k row.
K 3 rows.
Change to contrasting colour and work 2 rows in st-st.
Change to garment colour and cont in st-st until work measures 15cm/6in.
shape shoulders
Cast/bind off 5 sts at beg next 2 rows.
Cast/bind off

girl sleeves (both alike)

With 4mm(US 6) needles and garment colour, cast on 18 sts and k 3 rows.
Change to contrasting colour and work 2 rows in st-st beg with a k row.
Change to garment colour, k 1 row and then work 6 rows in st-st beg with a k row.
Cast/bind off.

girl head

With 4mm (US 6) needles and face colour, cast on 24
sts and work 2 rows in st-st.

3rd row *K2, inc, k1* to end. 30 sts.

4th–16th rows St-st.

shape top of head

17th row *K3, k2tog* to end.

18th row P.

19th row *K2, k2tog* to end.

20th row P.

21st row *K1, k2tog* to end.

22nd row *P2tog* to end.

Break yarn, leaving a long end and thread this through
remaining sts. Pull sts together tightly and fasten
securely. Join seam down to cast-on edge.

boy body

With 4mm (US 6) needles and garment colour, cast on
26 sts and k 3 rows.

Change to st-st and work 26 rows, dec 1st st at each
end of 7th and 17th rows while at the same time
maintaining the following stripe sequence:

Work 4 rows garment colour, then work 2 rows
contrasting colour.

Work 6 rows garment colour, then work 2 rows
contrasting colour.

These last 8 rows form the main stripe sequence.

27th row Cast on 4 sts, k to end.

28th row Cast on 4 sts, k2, p to last 2 sts, k2

29th–34th rows Work in st-st maintaining the stripe
sequence and the k2 edges on all rows.

35th row K9, cast/bind off 12 sts, k9.

36th row K2, p7, cast on 12 sts, p7, k2.

37th–42nd rows Work in st-st maintaining the stripe
sequence and the k2 edges on all rows.

43rd–44th rows Cast/bind off 4 sts, work to end.

45th–68th rows Work in st-st, inc 1 st at each end of
53rd and 63rd rows and maintaining stripe sequence.

69th–72nd rows K.

Cast/bind off.

boy head

Work as for Girl Head.

to finish

girl

Join shoulder seams of garment. Fold sleeves in half
lengthways and pin to garment, centre of cast/bind-off
edge to shoulder seam, and sew into place. Join side
and underarm seams. Attach head to neck of garment,
head seam to centre back.

Embroider facial features using darning needle. Add
hair by cutting long strands of yarn and forming them
into a bunch. Sew and secure the midpoint of the
strands to the middle of the head, to cover the top and
sides of the head but not the front or back. Sew and
secure the bunches in position at the sides of the head.

boy

Join side and underarm seams. Attach head to neck of
garment, head seam to centre back. Embroider facial
features using darning needle. Add hair by cutting
strands of long strands of yarn and forming them into a
bunch. Sew and secure the midpoint of the strands to
the middle of the head.

toddler knits

angel dress

A delightful dress that will make every little girl look like an angel. It feels gorgeous in sumptuous silk and is great for christenings, weddings or any other special occasion.

materials

3(3) 50g/1¾oz balls Jaeger *Silk* in pale blue/Blue Lily 128
Pair each of 2¾mm(US 2) and 3mm(US 2–3) knitting needles
Circular 2¾mm(US 2) knitting needle
1 small button

sizes

to fit

3–6	9–12	mths

actual measurements

chest

47	52	cm
18½	20½	in

length to shoulder

36	41	cm
14	16	in

tension/gauge

28 sts and 38 rows to 10cm/4in over st-st using 3mm(US 2–3) needles

abbreviations

alt alternate; **beg** begin(ning); **cm** centimetre(s); **cont** continue; **dec** decreas(e)(ing); **foll(s)** follow(s)(ing); **in** inch(es); **k** knit; **k2tog** knit next 2 sts together; **mm** millimetre; **p** purl; **psso** pass slipped stitch over; **rem** remain(ing); **rep** repeat; **RS** right side; **s1** slip one stitch; **skpo** s1, k1, psso; **st(s)** stitch(es); **st-st** stocking/stockinette stitch; **WS** wrong side; **yo (yarn over needle)** take yarn over right needle to make a st

back

**With 3mm(US 2–3) needles, cast on 124(132) sts.
K 2 rows.

Beg with a k row, work 6(8) rows in st-st.

Dec row (RS) K13(14), skpo, k to last 15(16) sts,
k2tog, k13(14).

Work 5(7) rows in st-st.

Rep the last 6(8) rows until 100(110) sts rem.

Cont straight until back measures 23(27)cm/9(10½)in
from cast-on edge, ending with a p row.

Dec row (RS) K3(5), [k2tog, k1] 32(34) times,
k1(3). 68(76) sts.

Cont in st-st without shaping until back measures
26(30)cm/10¼(11¾)in from cast-on edge, ending with
a p row.

shape armholes

Cast/bind off 6 sts at beg of next 2 rows. 56(64) sts.

Cast/bind off 5 sts at beg of next 2 rows. 46(54) sts.

Dec 1 st at each end of the next row and every foll alt
row until 36(42) sts rem.

P 1 row.**

back opening

Next row (RS) K17(20), turn and work on these sts
only for first side of back opening.

Next row Cast on 2 sts, k these 2 sts, then p to end.
19(22) sts.

Cont in st-st with 2 sts at centre back worked as k2 on
every row, until back measures 33(38)cm/13(15)in from
cast-on edge, ending with a p row.

shape neck

Next row (RS) K to last 7(9) sts, leave these sts on a
holder, turn.

Cont in st-st dec 1 st at neck edge on every row until 6(8)
sts rem.

Cont straight until back measures 36(41)cm/14¼(16)in
from cast-on edge, ending with a p row.

shape shoulder

Cast/bind off.

With RS facing, rejoin yarn to rem sts, k to end.

Cont in st-st with 2 sts at centre back worked as k2 on
every row, until back measures 33(38)cm/13(15)in from
cast-on edge ending with a p row.

shape neck

Next row (RS) K7(9), leave sts on a holder, k to end.

Cont in st-st dec 1 st at neck edge on every row until 6(8)
sts rem.

Cont straight until back measures 36(41)cm/14¼(16)in
from cast-on edge, ending with a p row.

shape shoulder

Cast/bind off.

front

Work as given for Back from ** to **.

shape neck

Next row (RS) K13(15) sts, turn and work on these sts
only for first side of neck shaping.

Dec 1 st at neck edge on every foll alt row until 6(8) sts
rem.

Cont without further shaping until front measures same
as Back to Shoulder, ending at side edge.

shape shoulder

Cast/bind off.

With RS facing, slip centre 10(12) sts onto a holder,
rejoin yarn to rem sts, k to end.

Complete to match first side, reversing shaping.

neckband

Join shoulder seams.

With RS facing and 2¾mm(US 2) circular needle, slip 7(9) sts from left back onto needle, pick up and k 11 sts up left back to shoulder, k 25(28) sts down left front neck, k across 10(12) sts from front neck holder, pick up and k 25(28) sts up right front neck to shoulder, k 11 sts from right back neck, k across 7(9) sts on back neck holder. 96(108) sts.

Work backwards and forwards in rows.

K 1 row.

Next row (buttonhole row) K1, yf, k2tog, k to end.

Next row (picot cast/bind-off row) (WS) Working knitwise, cast/bind off 3 sts, *slip st from right needle back onto left needle, cast on 2 sts, cast/bind off 5 sts: rep from * to end.

armbands

Join left shoulder and neckband seam.

With RS facing and 2¾mm(US 2) needles, pick up and k 84(88) sts evenly around armhole edge.

K 2 rows.

Cast/bind off knitwise.

lower edging

Join left side and armband seam. With RS facing and 2¾mm(US 2) circular needle, pick up and k 246(262) sts around lower edge of back and front.

Next row (picot cast/bind-off row) (WS) Working knitwise, cast/bind off 2 sts, *slip st from right needle back onto left needle, cast on 2 sts, cast/bind off 5 sts, rep from * to end, ending the last rep with cast/bind-off rem sts.

to finish

Join right side and armband seam. Overlap bands at centre back opening. Sew on button.

snowflake hat and scarf

This hat and scarf looks great in a variety of colourways – so why not make one to match your child's coat. Perfect for days in the snow or just out and about with mummy.

materials

2 50g/1¾oz balls of Jaeger *Matchmaker Merino DK* in main colour **M** (red/Cherry 656) or (blue/Pacific) and 2 balls in **A** (cream/Cream 662)

Pair each of 3¾mm(US 5) and 4mm(US 6) knitting needles

Spare knitting needles

sizes

to fit

1	2	3
6mths–1yr	1–2	2–3yrs

tension/gauge

22 sts and 30 rows to 10cm/4in over st-st using 4mm(US 6) needles

abbreviations

cm centimetre(s); **cont** continue; **foll(s)** follow(s)(ing); **inc** increas(e)(ing); **in** inch(es); **k** knit; **k2tog** knit next 2 sts together; **mm** millimetre(s); **p** purl; **p2tog** purl next 2 sts together; **rem** remain(ing); **rep** repeat; **RS** right side; **st(s)** stitch(es); **st-st** stocking/stockinette stitch

note

When working from chart, use separate small balls of yarn for each colour area and twist yarns at colour change to avoid holes.

hat

With 4mm(US 6) needles and M, cast on 7 (9:11) sts.
Work in st-st beg with a k row and 2-row stripes as folls:

1st row With M, k, inc 1 st at each end of row. 9(11:13) sts.

2nd row With M, p, inc 1 st at each end of row. 11(13:15) sts.

3rd row With A, k.

4th row With A, p, inc 1 st at each end of row. 13(15:17) sts.

5th row With M, k,inc 1 st at each end of row. 15(17:19) sts.

6th row With M,p.

7th row With A, k, inc 1 st at each end of row. 17(19:21) sts.

8th row With A, p.

9th–14th (16th:18th) rows Work in st-st without shaping keeping stripe pattern correct.

Leave sts on spare needle.

Make second earflap to match.

With 3¾mm(US 5) needles and M, cast on 12(13:17) sts, k across 17(19:21) sts of first ear flap, cast on 32(36:44) sts, k across 17(19:21) sts of second ear flap, cast on 12(13:17) sts. 90(100:120) sts.

Work 3 rows in st-st, starting with a p row.

Change to 4mm(US 6) needles and work snowflake motif as folls:

1st row K38(43:53), work 14 sts from 1st row of snowflake chart, k38(43:53).

2nd row P38(43:53), work 14 sts from 2nd row of snowflake chart, p38(43:53).

3rd–16th rows Complete all 16 rows of chart.

Work a further 2(4:6) rows in st-st in M.

shape top (all sizes)

1st row K.

2nd row *P2tog, p8, rep from * to end. 81(90:108) sts.

3rd row K.

4th row P.

5th row *K7, k2tog, rep from * to end. 72(80:96) sts.

6th row P.

7th row K.

8th row *P2tog, p6, rep from * to end. 63(70:84) sts.

9th row K.

10th row P.

11th row *K5, k2tog, rep from * to end. 54 (60:72) sts.

size 1

12th row *P4, p2tog, rep from * to end. 45 sts.

13th row *K3, k2tog rep from * to end. 36 sts.

14th row *P2tog rep from * to end. 18 sts.

15th row *K2tog, rep from * to end. 9 sts.

size 2

12th row P.

13th row *K4, k2tog, rep from * to end. 50 sts.

14th row P.

15th row *K3, k2tog, rep from * to end. 40 sts.
16th row *P2tog, rep from * to end. 20 sts.
17th row *K2tog, rep from * to end. 10 sts.
size 3
12th row P.
13th row *K4, k2tog, rep from * to end. 60 sts.
14th row P.
15th row *K3, k2tog, rep from * to end. 48 sts.
16th row P.
17th row *K2, k2tog, rep from * to end. 36 sts.
18th row *P2tog, p1, rep from * to end. 24 sts.
19th row *K2tog, rep from * to end. 12 sts.
all sizes
Thread yarn through rem sts, draw up tightly and
fasten off securely

edging

With RS facing, 3¾mm(US 5) needles and M, pick up
and k 12(14:17) sts from back cast-on edge, 31(37:43)
sts around ear flap, 32(36:44) sts from front cast-on
edge, 31(37:43) sts around ear flap and 12(14:17) sts
from back cast-on edge. 118(136:164) sts.
Cast/bind off knitwise.

to finish

Join back seam. Weave in loose ends. Cut three
60cm/24in lengths of M. Thread half the length
through bottom centre of ear flap. Taking one end from
front and one end from back, make a plait with two
ends per strand. Knot at end and trim. Rep for second
earflap.

scarf

With 4mm(US 6) needles and M, cast on 32 sts.
Work 4 rows in st-st.
5th row (place motif) K9, work 1st row of chart, k9.
Cont to completion of chart. Work 4 more rows.
Change to stripes of *2 rows A, 2 rows M* until scarf
measures 120cm/46in, ending with 2 rows A.
Work 4 more rows in M then work chart again, but
this time turn it upside down and work 16th–1st rows
in intarsia.

Work 4 rows in M.
Cast/bind off.

edgings

With 3¾mm(US 5) needles and A, pick up and k 32 sts at
end of scarf.
Cast/bind off knitwise.
Repeat for other end.
With 33/4mm(US 5) needles and A, pick up and k 276 sts
along scarf.
Cast/bind off knitwise.
Repeat for other side.

finishing

Weave in loose ends. Neaten scarf corners.

snowflake motif

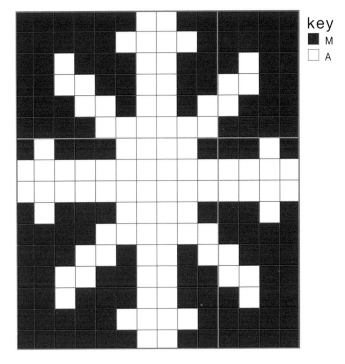

key
■ M
□ A

luxury lettered coat

A bold woolly knit that is great fun to wear and educational, too! Have fun helping your child find their own initials or spell out the letters in their name.

materials

2 balls of Rowan *Yorkshire Tweed DK* main colour **M** (bright blue/ Slosh 345) and 1 ball in each of (red/Scarlet 344), (purple/Revel 342), (dark blue/Champion 346), (green/Frog 349), (yellow/Lime Leaf 348), (turquoise/Skip 347) and (pale pink/Frolic 350)
Pair each of 3mm(US 2–3) and 3¾mm(US 5) knitting needles
5 buttons

sizes

to fit

6–12 mths	1–2	2–3	yrs
actual measurements			
chest			
56	63	70	cm
22	24¾	27½	in
back length			
32	37	41	cm
12½	14½	16	in
sleeve seam			
15	19	21.5	cm
6	7½	8½	in

tension/gauge

23 sts and 32 rows to 10cm/4in over st-st using 3¾mm(US 5) needles

abbreviations

cm centimetre(s); **foll(s)** follow(s)(ing); **in** inch(es); **k** knit; **k2tog** knit next 2 sts together; **mm** millimetre(s); **p** purl; **st(s)** stitch(es); **st-st** stocking/stockinette stitch; **yo (yarn over needle)** take yarn over right needle to make a st

note

When working from chart, use separate small balls of yarn for each colour area and twist yarns at colour change to avoid holes.

back

With 3mm(US 2–3) needles and M, cast on 64(72:80) sts.

1st row *K, p1, rep from * to end.
2nd row *P1, k1, rep from * to end.
Work 6 rows more in moss/seed st.
Change to 3¾mm(US 5) needles and st-st.
Using intarsia method, foll chart.

left front

With 3mm(US 2–3) needles and M, cast on 32(36:40) sts.
Work 8 rows in moss/seed st as given for back.
Change to 3¾mm(US 5) needles and st-st.
Using intarsia method, foll chart.

right front

Work as given for Left Front, foll the correct chart.

sleeves

With 3mm(US 2–3) needles and M, cast on 32(34:34) sts.
Work 8 rows in moss/seed st as given for back.
Change to 3¾mm(US 5) needles and st-st.
Using intarsia method, foll chart.

button band

With 3mm(US 2–3) needles and M, cast on 6 sts.
Work in moss/seed st as given for back until band, when slightly stretched, fits from cast on edge to neck of Left Front.
Cast/bind off.
Sew Button Band to Left Front.
Mark positions for 5 buttons, the first 1cm/¾in from cast-on edge, the fifth 1cm/¾in from top of band, the rem 3 evenly spaced between.

buttonhole band

Work as for Button Band, making buttonholes as moss/seed st 2 sts, k2tog, yo, moss/seed 2 sts, where marked on Button Band.
Sew band to Right Front.

collar

Join shoulder seams.
With 3mm(US 2–3) needles and M, and starting and finishing halfway across front bands, pick up and k 22(25:26) sts from right front neck, 24(26:28) sts from back neck and 22(25:26) sts from left front neck. 68(76:80).
Work 6cm/2¼in in moss/seed stitch as given for back.
Cast/bind off loosely.

to finish

Pin sleeves to body, centre of sleeve top to shoulder seam and stitch. Join underarm and side seams. Weave in loose ends. Sew on buttons.

lettered coat chart: size 1

key
- M
- red
- purple
- dark blue
- green
- yellow
- pale pink

size 1 sleeve

size 1 sleeve

key

- M
- red
- purple
- dark blue
- green
- yellow
- turquoise
- pale pink

112
110

100

90

80

70

60

50

40

30

20

10

1

size 3
size 2
sizes 2 and 3 sleeve
sizes 2 and 3 sleeve
size 2
size 3

head honcho poncho

This stripy poncho is eye-catching and fun to wear. The simple design makes it easy to take on and off and it's very fashionable, too.

materials

2(3:4) Jaeger *Matchmaker Merino DK* in (orange/Pumpkin 898) and 2(3:4) in (pink/Rock Rose 896), 2(2:2) in (blue/Pacific 889), 2(2:2) in (purple/Azalea 897)

2(2:2) Jaeger *Baby Merino DK* in (red/Red 231) and 2(2:2) in (yellow/Gold 225)

Pair each of 3¼mm(US 3) and 3¾mm(US 5) knitting needles

Spare knitting needle

Crochet hook

1 button

sizes

To fit

6–12 mths	1–2	2–3	yrs
actual measurements			
chest			
51	55	61	cm
20	21½	24	in
back length			
32	37	41	cm
12½	14½	16	in
wingspan			
61	76	85	cm
24	30	33½	in

tension/gauge

23 sts and 32 rows to 10cm/4in over st-st using 3¾mm(US 5) needles

abbreviations

alt alternate; **beg** begin(ning); **cm** centimetre(s); **cont** continue; **dec** decreas(e)(ing); **foll(s)** follow(s)(ing); **inc** increas(e)(ing); **in** inch(es); **k** knit; **k2tog** knit next 2 sts together; **mm** millimetre; **p** purl; **p2tog** purl next 2 sts together; **patt** pattern; **PM** place marker(s); **psso** pass slipped stitch over; **rem** remain(ing); **rep** repeat; **RS** right side; **skpo** s1, k1, psso; **s1** slip next stitch; **st(s)** stitch(es); **st-st** stocking/stockinette stitch; **WS** wrong side; **yo (yarn over needle)** take yarn over right needle to make a st

back

With 3¾mm(US 5) needles and A, cast on 192(228:264) sts.

1st row *K1, p1, rep from * to end.

2nd row *P1, p1, rep from * to end.

Cont in moss/seed st as follows:

3rd row *Dec, moss/seed st 92(110:128), dec, rep from * once. 188(224:260) sts.

4th and alternate rows Moss/seed st without shaping.

5th row Moss/seed st 92(110:128), dec, dec, moss/seed st 92(110:128). 186(222:258) sts.

7th row *Dec, moss/seed st 89(107:125), dec, rep from * once.

9th row Moss/seed st 89(107:125), dec, dec moss/seed st 89(107:125). 180(216:244) sts.

11th row *Dec, moss/seed st 86(104:122), dec, rep from * once.

13th row Change to Pink and st-st, *k2tog, k84(102:120) skpo, rep from * once.

14th and alternate rows P.

15th row K2tog, *k26(32:38), skpo, rep from * twice, **k2tog, k26(32:38), rep from ** twice, skpo. 164(200:236) sts.

17th row *K2tog, k78(96:114), skpo, rep from * once. 160(196:232) sts.

19th row K2tog, *k24(30:36), skpo, rep from * twice, **k2tog, k24(30:36), rep from ** twice, skpo. 152(188:224) sts.

21st row *K2tog, k72(90:108), skpo, rep from * once. 148(184:220) sts.

23rd row K2tog, *k22(28:34), skpo, rep from * twice, **k2tog, k22(28:34), rep from ** twice, skpo. 140(176:212) sts.

25th row Change to Red, *k2tog, *k66(84:102), skpo, rep from * once. 136(172:208) sts.

Cont dec as established (8 sts on one row, 4 sts on foll row), changing to Yellow on row 37, Blue on row 49, Purple on row 61, and then starting the colour repeat again, until the 65th(77th:89th) rows when16 sts rem. PM at each end of row for back neck.

Next row P.

All sizes on 16 sts.

1st row *K2tog, skpo, rep from * 3 times. 8 sts.

2nd and 4th rows P.

3rd row K2tog, skpo, rep from * once. 4 sts.
Cast/bind off.

front

Work as Back until completion of 60th(72nd:84th) row. 32 sts.

shape neck

1st row Cast/bind off 4 sts, k10, skpo, k2tog, k14. 26 sts.

2nd row Cast/bind off 4 sts, p to end. 22 sts.

3rd row Cast/bind off 4 sts, k5, skpo, k2tog, k9. 16 sts.

4th row Cast/bind off 2 sts, p to end. 12 sts.

5th row Cast/bind off 2 sts, k2, skpo, k2tog, k4. 8 sts.

6th row Cast/bind off 2 sts, p to end. 6 sts.
Cast/bind off.

neckband

Join right shoulder seam.

With 3¼mm(US 3) needles and Pink, pick up and k 32 sts from front neck and 24 sts from back neck between markers. 56 sts.

Work 5 rows in moss/seed st as given for back.

Cast/bind off in moss/seed st.

Join left shoulder seam, leaving 7cm/2¾in open at neck edge.

With RS facing and with 3¼mm(US 3) needles and Pink, pick up and k 50 sts around opening.

Next row (buttonhole row) Moss/seed 2 sts, p2tog, yo, moss/seed to end.

Cast/bind off in moss/seed st.

to finish

Sew on button. Weave in any loose ends.

fringe

Cut yarns into 15cm/6in lengths. With 3 lengths together, fold in half and, using a crochet hook, pull fold through cast-on knitting. Pull the ends through the loop and pull tight. Attach fringe around cast-on edge of poncho at intervals and in colours of your choice.

a boy's own jacket

A great jacket for winter days. The snuggly yarn will keep the chill out and keep your little one warm and toasty even in the coldest weather.

materials

3(3:3) 50g/1¾oz balls of Rowan *Calmer* in each of **A** (pale blue/ Calmer 463) and **B** (dark blue/ Slosh 479)
Pair of 5mm(US 8) knitting needles
Stitch holders
30(30:35)cm/12(12:14)in chunky open-ended zip fastener

sizes

to fit

6–12mths	1–2	2–3	yrs

actual measurements

chest

58	63	68	cm
23	24¾	26¾	in

length to shoulder

30	33	36	cm
11¾	13	14¼	in

sleeve seam

18	21	23	cm
7	8¼	9	in

tension/gauge

21 sts and 30 rows to 10cm/4in over st-st using 5mm(US 8) needles

abbreviations

alt alternate; **beg** begin(ning); **cm** centimetre(s); **cont** continue; **dec** decreas(e)(ing); **foll(s)** follow(s)(ing); **in** inch(es); **inc** increas(e)(ing); **k** knit; **k2tog** knit next 2 sts together; **k3tog** knit next 3 sts together; **m1** make one st by picking up and working into the back of the loop lying between last sts and next st; **mm** millimetre(s); **p** purl; **PM** place marker; **psso** pass slipped stitch over; **rem** remain(ing); **rep** repeat; **RS** right side; **s1** slip one stitch; **skpo** s1, k1, psso; **st(s)** stitch(es); **st-st** stocking/stockinette stitch; **WS** wrong side

back

With 5mm(US 8) needles and A, cast on 62(66:70) sts.

1st row (RS) K2, *p2, k2, rep from * to end.

2nd row (WS) P2, *k2, p2, rep from * to end.

Rep these 1st and 2nd rows for 4cm/1½in, ending with a 1st row.

Next row (WS) P.

Beg with a k (RS) row, work in st-st in 8-row stripes of B and A, until back measures 17(19:21)cm/6¾(7½:8¼)in from beg, ending with a p row.

shape armholes

Cast/bind off 5 sts at beg of next 2 rows. 52(56:60) sts.

Cont straight, keeping stripe patt correct, until back measures 30(33:36)cm/11¾(13:14¼)in from beg, ending with a p row.

shape shoulders

Cast/bind off 15(16:17) sts at beg of next 2 rows. Leave rem 22(24:26) sts on a holder.

left front

With 5mm(US 8) needles and A, cast on 31(33:35) sts.

1st row *K2, p2, rep from * to last 3(1:3) sts, k3(1:3).

2nd row K1, p2(0:2), *k2, p2, rep from * to end.

Rep these 2 rows for 4cm/1½in, ending with a 1st row.

Next row (WS) K1, p to end.

Beg with a k (RS) row, work in st-st in 8-row stripes of B and A, working 1 st at front edge as a k st on every row.

Work straight until front measures 6(7:8)cm/2¼(2¾:3)in from beg, ending with a p row.

work pocket

Next row K10(11:12), turn and leave rem sts on first holder, cast on 18 sts, p to end.

Cont in st-st keeping striped patt correct on these 28(29:30) sts only and work a further 19 rows, so ending with a k row.

Next row Cast/bind off 18 sts, leave rem 10(11:12) sts on second holder.

With RS facing, rejoin yarn to 21(22:23) sts on first holder, k to end.

Keeping 1 st at front edge as a k st on every row, work

20 rows in striped st-st.

Next row (WS) K1, p20(21:22), p across 10(11:12) sts on second holder.

Cont straight, keeping 1 st at front edge as a k st on every row, until right front measures 17(19:21)cm/6¾(7½:8¼)in from beg, ending with a p row.

shape armhole

Cast/bind off 5 sts at beg of next row. 26(28:30) sts.

Cont straight until work is 7(9:11) rows less than back at shoulder.

shape neck

1st row WS facing, cast/bind off 4 sts, p to last st, k1.

2nd row K, PM at neck edge.

3rd row Cast/bind off 4 sts, p to last st, k1.

4th and alt rows K.

5th row Cast/bind off 2 sts, work to end.

7th row Cast/bind off 1 st, work to end.

2nd size only

Rep 6th and 7th rows once.

3rd size only

Rep 6th and 7th rows twice.

all sizes

Next row Cast/bind off.

right front

With 5mm(US 8) needles and A, cast on 31(33:35) sts.

1st row (RS) K3(1:3), *p2, k2, rep from * to end.

2nd row (WS) *P2, k2, rep from * to last 3(1:3) sts, p2(0:2), k1.

Rep these 2 rows for 4cm/1½in, ending with a 1st row.

Next row (WS) P to last st, k1.

Beg with a k (RS) row, work in st-st in 8-row stripes of B and A, working 1 st at front edge as a k st on every row.

Work straight until front measures 6(7:8)cm/2¼(2¾:3)in from beg, ending with a p row.

work pocket

Next row (RS) K21(22:23), turn and leave rem 10(11:12) sts on first holder.

Beg with a p row and keeping 1 st at front edge as a k st on every row, work 20 rows in striped st-st.

Leave sts on second holder.

With RS facing, rejoin yarn to 10(11:12) sts on first holder and cast on 18 sts, k these sts then k across 10(11:12) sts on first holder. 28(29:30) sts.

Work 19 rows in striped st-st, so ending with a p row.

Next row (RS) Cast/bind off 18 sts, k to end.

Next row P10(11:12), then work across 21(22:23) sts on second holder as p20(21:22), k1. 31(33:35) sts.

Cont straight, keeping 1 st at front edge as a k st on every row, until left front measures 17(19:21)cm/6¾(7½:8¼)in from beg, ending with a k row.

shape armhole

Cast/bind off 5 sts at beg of next row.

Cont straight until work is 8(10:12) rows less than back at shoulder.

shape neck

Work to match left front starting with RS facing.

hood

Join shoulder seams.

With RS facing and with 5mm(US 8) needles and A, starting at PM pick up and k 14(16:18) sts from right front neck, k across 22(24:26) sts of back neck, pick up and k 14(16:18) sts from left front neck, ending at PM. Working in st-st, beg with a p row, and 8-row stripes as before, continue as follows. Inc on given rows **only**.

4th row K23(26:29), m1, k4, m1, k23(26:29). 52(58:764) sts.

8th(10th and 12th) row K23(26:29), m1, k6, m1, k23(26:29). 54(60:66) sts.

12th(16th and 20th) row K23(26:29), m1, k8, m1, k23(26:29). 56(62:68) sts.

16th(20th and 26th) row K23(26:29), m1, k10, m1, k23(26:29). 58(64:70) sts.

Cont inc as established on every foll 4th row to 68(74:80) sts.

Work 13 rows without shaping.

shape top

Dec on given rows **only**.

1st row K31(34:37), k2tog, k2, skpo, k31(34:37). 66(72:78) sts.

5th row K30(33:36), k2tog, k2, skpo, k30(33:36). 64(70:76 sts).

9th row K29(32:35), k2tog, k2, skpo, k29(32:35). 62(68:74) sts.

Cont to dec as established on alt rows to 54(60:66) sts.

Next row P.

Next row K23(26:29), k3tog, k2, skpo, k23(26:29). 50(56:62) sts.

Next row P.

Cast/bind off.

sleeves

With 5mm(US 8) needles and A, cast on 28(28:32) sts.

1st row (RS) K1, *p2, k2, rep from * to last 3 sts, p2, k1.

2nd row (WS) P1, *k2, p2, rep from * to last 3 sts, k2, p1.

Rep these 2 rows for 4cm/1½in, ending with a 1st row.

Next row (WS) P.

Beg with a k (RS) row, work in st-st in 4-row stripes of B and A throughout, **at the same time**, inc 1 st at each end of 3rd and every foll 3rd row until there are 54(58:64) sts.

Cont straight until sleeve measures 18(21:23)cm/7(8¼:9)in from beg, PM at each end of last row, then work 7 more rows.

Cast/bind off.

hood edging

Fold cast/bind-off edge of hood in half and join seam. With RS facing, 5mm(US 8) needles and A, pick up 2 sts per 3 rows around edge of hood.

Work 5 rows in k2, p2 rib as given for Back.

Cast/bind off in rib.

pocket edgings

With RS facing, 5mm(US 8) needles and A, pick up and k18 along edge of each pocket.

Beg with a 2nd row, work 3 rows in k2, p2 rib as given for Back.

Cast/bind off in rib.

to finish

Sew row ends of hood edging to cast/bind-off sts at front edges. With centre of cast/bind-off edge of sleeve to shoulder, sew sleeves into armholes, with row ends above PM sewn to sts cast/bind off at underarm. Join side seams and sleeve seams. Hand-sew zip fastener to front edges. Slipstitch pocket linings in place.

fancy fair isle

Taking a modern twist on a classic design, this cardigan has mother-of-pearl buttons and looks extremely cute with the matching hat.

materials

4(4:4) 50g/1¾oz balls of Jaeger *Matchmaker Merino* 4 ply in **M** (cream/Ash 731), and 1 ball in each of (ecru/Snowdrop 102), (pale green/Thyme 715), (aqua green/Mineral 741), (pale pink/Cyclamen 694), and (dark pink/Strawberry 633)
Pair of 3¼mm(US 3) knitting needles
5 mother-of-pearl buttons

sizes

cardigan to fit

6–12 mths	1–2	2–3	yrs
actual measurements			
chest			
56	61	66	cm
22	24	26	in
length			
30	33	36	cm
12	13	14	in
sleeve length			
18	21	23	cm
7	8¼	9	in
hat to fit			
6–12 mths	1–2	2–3	yrs

tension/gauge

28 sts and 36 rows to 10cm/4in over st-st using 3¼mm(US 3) needles

abbreviations

alt alternate; **beg** begin(ning); **cm** centimetre(s); **cont** continue; **foll(s)** follow(s)(ing); **in** inch(es); **inc** increas(e)(ing); **k** knit; **k2tog** knit next 2 sts together; **mm** millimetre(s); **p** purl; **patt** pattern; **PM** place marker; **rem** remain(ing); **rep** repeat; **RS** right side; **st(s)** stitch(es); **st-st** stocking/stockinette stitch; **WS** wrong side; **yo (yarn over needle)** take yarn over right needles to make a st

note

When working from chart, strand yarn not in use across WS of work, weaving in where it crosses more than 4 sts.

back

With 3¼mm(US 3) needles and M, cast on 77(85:93) sts.

1st row (RS) K1, *p1, k1, rep from * to end.
2nd row (WS) P1, *k1, p1, rep from * to end.
Rep these 2 rows for 3cm/1¼in, ending with a 2nd row.
Beg with a k (RS) row, work 4 rows in st-st.
Now work 29 rows in st-st from Fair Isle chart, working between lines for correct size.
Cont in st-st in M only until back measures 17(19:21)cm/7(7½:8¼)in from cast-on edge, ending with a p row.

shape armholes

Cast/bind off 5 sts at beg of next 2 rows. 67(75:83) sts.
Cont straight until back measures 30(33:36)cm/11¾(13:14¼)in, ending with a p row.

shape shoulders

Cast/bind off 20(22:24) sts at beg of next 2 rows.
Leave rem 27(31:35) sts on a holder.

left front

** With 3¼mm(US 3) needles and M, cast on 37(41:45) sts and work 3cm/1¼in in k1, p1 rib as given for the Back ending with a 2nd row.
Beg with a k row, work 4 rows in st-st.
Now work 29 rows in st-st from Fair Isle chart, working between lines for correct size and garment piece.
Cont in st-st in M only until left front measures 17(19:21)cm/6¾(7½:8¼)in from cast-on edge, ending with a p row.**

shape armhole

Cast/bind off 5 sts at beg of next row. 32(36:40) sts.
Cont straight until left front measures 24(27:30)cm/9½(10½:11¾)in from cast-on edge, ending with a k row.

shape neck

1st row Cast/bind off 3 sts, p to end. 29(33:37) sts.
2nd row K.
3rd row Cast/bind off 2 sts, p to end. 27(31:35) sts.
Repeat 2nd and 3rd rows 2(3:4) times. 23(25:27) sts.
Next row K.

Next row Cast/bind off 1 st, p to end. 22(24:26) sts.
Repeat the last 2 rows twice. 20(22:24) sts.
Cont without shaping until left front matches Back to shoulder, ending at side edge.
Cast/bind off.

right front

Work as given for Left Front from ** to **.
Next row K.

shape armhole

Cast/bind off 5 sts at beg of next row. 32(36:40) sts.
Cont straight until right front measures 24(27:30)cm/9½(10½:11¾)in from cast-on edge, ending with a p row.

shape neck

1st row Cast/bind off 3 sts, k to end. 29 (33:37) sts.
2nd row P.
3rd row Cast/bind off 2 sts, k to end. 27(31:35) sts.
Repeat 2nd and 3rd rows 2(3:4) times. 23(25:27) sts.
Next row P.
Next row Cast/bind off 1 st, k to end. 22(24:26) sts.
Repeat the last 2 rows twice. 20(22:24) sts.
Cont without shaping until right front matches Back to shoulder, ending at side edge.
Cast/bind off.

sleeves

With 3¼mm(US 3) needles and M, cast on 37(41:45) sts and work 3cm/1¼in in k1, p1 rib as given for the Back, ending with a 2nd row.
Beg with a k (RS) row, work 4 rows in st-st.
Now work 19 rows from sleeve chart, working between lines for correct size, **at the same time**, inc and take into patt, 1 st at each end of 3rd and every foll 3rd row until there are 67(71:77) sts.
Cont straight until sleeve measures 18(21:23)cm/7(8¼:9)in from cast-on edge, PM at each end of last row.
Work 6 more rows.
Cast/bind off.

button band

Join shoulder seams.

With RS facing, 3¼mm(US 3) needles and M, pick up and k 61(67:73) sts up left front edge.

Beg with a 2nd row, work 7 rows in k1, p1 rib as given for Back.

Cast/bind off in rib.

Mark positions for 5 buttons, the first to come 1cm/⅜in above lower edge, the 5th to come in the neckband, with rem 3 spaced evenly between.

buttonhole band

With RS facing, 3¼mm(US 3) needles and M, pick up and k 61(67:73) sts up right front edge.

Beg with a 2nd row, work 3 rows in k1, p1 rib as given for Back.

Next row (buttonhole row) (RS) [K1, p1] twice, [k2tog, yo, rib14(14:16)] 3 times, k2tog, yo, rib to end.

Work 3 more rows in rib.

Cast/bind off in rib.

neckband

With RS facing, 3¼mm(US 3) needles and M, pick up and k 28 sts up buttonhole band and right neck, k across 27(31:35) sts at back neck, then pick up and k 28 sts down left front neck and button band. 83(87:91) sts.

Beg with a 2nd row, work 1 row in k1, p1 rib as given for Back.

Next row (buttonhole row) (RS) K1, p1, k2tog, yo, rib to end.

Rib 5 more rows.

Cast/bind off rib.

to finish

With centre of cast/bind off edge of sleeve to shoulder, sew sleeves into armholes with row ends above markers sewn to cast/bound-off sts at underarm. Join side sleeve seams. Sew on buttons to correspond with buttonholes.

hat

With M, cast on 117(129:141) sts.

1st row (RS) K1, *p1, k1, rep from * to end.

2nd row P1, *k1, p1, rep from * to end.

Rep these 2 rows until work measures 9cm/3½in, ending with a 2nd row.

Beg with a k row, work 4(6:8) rows in st-st.

Cont in st-st and work 20 rows from chart, between lines for correct size.

Cont in A only and work 1(3:5) rows in st-st.

shape top

1st row (RS) K6, [k2tog, k4] 18(20:22) times, k2tog, k1. 98(108:118) sts.

Work 3 rows.

5th row (RS) K5, [k2tog, k3] 18(20:22) times, k2tog, k1. 79(87:95) sts.

Work 3 rows.

9th row K4, [k2tog, k2] 18(20:22) times, k2tog, k1. 60(66:72) sts.

Work 3 rows.

13th row K3, [k2tog, k1] 18(20:22) times, k2tog, k1. 41(45:49) sts.

Work 1(3:3) rows.

Next row K2, [k2tog] 18(20:22) times, k2tog, k1. 22(24:26) sts.

Work 1(1:3) rows.

Next row K1, [k2tog] 10(11:12) times, k1. 12(13:14) sts.

Next row P.

Next row [K2tog] 6(6:7) times, k0(1:0). 6(7:7) sts.

Break yarn.

to finish

Thread yarn through rem sts, pull up and join seam, reversing seam on last 5cm/2in of rib.

sleeve and hat chart

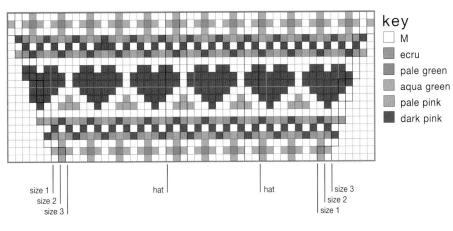

key
- ☐ M
- ▨ ecru
- ▨ pale green
- ▨ aqua green
- ▨ pale pink
- ▧ dark pink

size 1
size 2
size 3

hat   hat

size 3
size 2
size 1

jacket chart

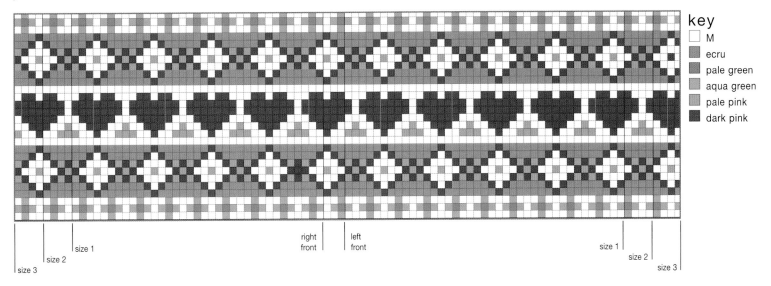

key
- ☐ M
- ▨ ecru
- ▨ pale green
- ▨ aqua green
- ▨ pale pink
- ▧ dark pink

size 3
size 2
size 1

right front   left front

size 1
size 2
size 3

1-2-3 sweater

Teach your child to count with this stripy sweater, which is ideal for a first day at nursery school. The cotton yarn makes it perfect for spring days or summer evenings.

materials

2(2:2) 50g/1¾oz balls of Rowan *Glacé* in **A** (blue/Splendour 810), 1(2:2) balls in each of **B** (turquoise/Pie 809), **C** (ecru/Ecru 725), **D** (mauve/Hyacinth 787) and **E** (yellow/Butter 795)
Pair of 3¾mm(US 5) knitting needles
Spare knitting needle
2 buttons

sizes

to fit

6–12 mths	1–2	2–3	yrs
actual measurements			
chest			
56	61	66	cm
22	24	26	in
length			
30	33	36	cm
11¾	13	14¾	in
sleeve seam			
18	21	23	cm
7	8¼	9	in

tension/gauge

23 sts and 32 rows to 10cm/4in over st-st using 3¾mm(US 5) needles

abbreviations

cm centimetre(s); **cont** continue; **foll(s)** follow(s)(ing); **in** inch(es); **inc** increas(e)(ing); **k** knit; **k2tog** knit next 2 sts together; **mm** millimetre(s); **p** purl; **PM** place markers; **rem** remain(ing); **rep** repeat(ing); **RS** right side; **st(s)** stitch(es); **st-st** stocking/stockinette stitch; **WS** wrong side; **yo (yarn over needle)** take yarn over right needle to make a st

note

When working from chart, use separate small balls of yarn for each colour area and twist yarns at colour change to avoid holes.

Beg with a k (RS) row, work 15 rows in st-st from chart for back working between lines for correct size.
Cont in st-st in stripe sequence as given until back measures 18(20:22)cm/7(7¾:8¾)in from cast-on edge, ending with a p row.

shape armholes

Cont in st-st and stripe sequence, cast/bind off 5(5:6) sts at beg of next 2 rows. 54(60:64) sts. **
Cont straight until back measures 30(33:36)cm/11¾(13:14¼)in, ending with a p row.

shape shoulders

1st row (RS) Cast/bind off 15(17:18) sts, k to end.
2nd row P15(17:18) sts, turn and cont on these sts only for shoulder button band and slip rem 24(26:28) sts onto a spare needle for back neck.
Next row (RS) K2, [p2, k2] 2(3:3) times, p2, k3(1:2).
Next row P3(1:2), [k2, p2] 3(4:4) times.
Rep the last 2 rows once more.
Cast off in rib.

front

Work as given for Back from ** to **, but work chart for front between lines for correct size.
Cont straight until 14(16:16) rows less than Back to shoulder have been worked, so ending with a p row.

shape neck

1st row (RS) K23(25:27), turn and cont on these sts only, leave rem sts on a holder.
2nd row Cast/bind off 2 sts, p to end. 21(23:25) sts.
3rd row K.
4th row Cast/bind off 2 sts, p to end. 19(21:23) sts.
5th–8th(8th:9th) rows Dec 1 st at beg of row, work to end. 15(17:18) sts.
Work 2(4:5) more rows in st-st.

buttonhole band

Next row (RS) K3(1:2), [p2, k2] 3(4:4) times.
Next row P2, [k2, p2] 2(3:3) times, k2, p3(1:2).
Next row (buttonhole row) K3(1:2), [p2, k2] 0(1:1) time, p2, k2tog, yo, [p2, k2] twice.
Next row P2, [k2, p2] 2(3:3) times, k2, p3(1:2).
Cast off in rib.
With RS facing, sl 8(10:10) sts at centre front onto a holder, rejoin yarn to rem sts from spare needle and k to end.

stripe sequence

*8 rows A, 8 rows B, 8 rows C, 8 rows D, 8 rows E, repeat from *.

back

**With 3¾mm(US 5) needles and A, cast on 64(70:76) sts.
1st row (RS) K1(2:1), p2, *k2, p2, rep from * to last 1(2:1) sts, k1(2:1).
2nd row (WS) P1(2:1), k2, *p2, k2, rep from * to last 1(2:1) sts, p1(2:1).
Rep 1st and 2nd rows 4 more times.

1st row P.
2nd row Cast/bind off 2 sts, k to end. 21(23:25) sts.
3rd row P.
4th row Cast/bind off 2 sts, k to end. 19(21:23) sts.
5th–8th(8th:9th) rows Dec 1 st at beg of row, work to end. 15(17:18) sts.
Work 6(8:8) more rows in st-st.
Cast/bind off.

sleeves

With 3¾mm(US 5) needles and A, cast on 34(34:38) sts.
1st row (RS) K2, *p2, k2, rep from * to end.
2nd row (WS) P2, *k2, p2, rep from * to end.
Rep these 2 rows 4 more times.
Beg with a k (RS) row, work 15 rows from chart between lines for correct size and garment piece, then cont in st-st in stripe sequence as before while **at the same time**, inc 1 st at each end of 3rd(3rd:3rd) row and every foll 3rd row until there are 56(60:64) sts.
Cont straight until sleeve measures 18(21:23)cm/7(8¼:9) in from cast-on edge, PM at each end of last row
Work 6(6:8) more rows.
Cast/bind off.

neckband

Join right shoulder seam.
With RS facing, 3¾mm(US 5) needles and A, pick up and k 20(22:24) sts down left front neck, k across 8(10:10) sts at centre front, pick up and k 18(20:20) sts up right front neck, then k across 24(26:28) sts at centre back. 70(76:86) sts.
1st row (WS) P2, *k2, p2, rep from * to end.
2nd row (RS) K2, *p2, k2, rep from * to end.
3rd row P2, *k2, p2, rep from * to end.
4th row (buttonhole row) K2, p2, k2tog, yo, *p2, k2, rep from * to end.
Work 3 rows in rib.
Cast/bind off in rib.

to finish

Overlap button band with buttonhole band and catch in place at armhole edge. With centre of cast/bound-edge of sleeve to shoulder, sew sleeves into armholes with row ends above markers sewn to cast/bound-off sts at underarm. Join side and sleeve seams. Sew buttons onto button band and neckband to correspond with buttonholes.

key
- A
- B
- C

numbers motif

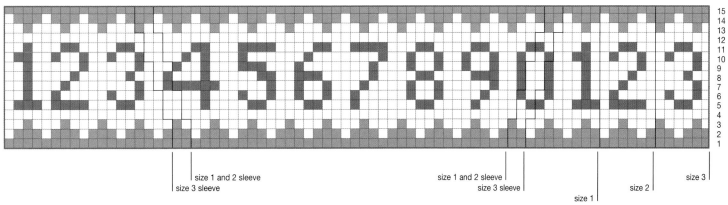

size 1 and 2 sleeve
size 3 sleeve
size 1 and 2 sleeve
size 3 sleeve
size 1
size 2
size 3

polka dot button-up

This spotted cardigan with its pretty picot edge looks equally great worn with jeans or with a favourite summer dress.

materials

4(5:5) 50g/1¾oz balls of Jaeger *Aqua Cotton* in **M** (dark pink/ India 322) and 1 ball in **A** (ecru/Creme 301)

Pair each of 3mm(US2–3) and 3¾mm(US 5) needles

Safety pin

5 buttons

sizes

to fit

6–12 mths	1–2	2–3	yrs
actual measurements			
chest			
56	63	70	cm
22	24¾	27½	in
back length			
32	37	41	cm
12½	14½	16	in
wingspan			
61	76	85	cm
24	30	33½	in

tension/gauge

23 sts and 32 rows to 10cm/4in over st-st using 3¾mm(US 5) needles

abbreviations

alt alternate; **beg** begin(ning); **cm** centimetre(s); **cont** continue; **dec** decreas(e)(ing); **foll(s)** follow(s)(ing); **inc** increas(e)(ing); **in** inch(es); **k** knit; **k2tog** knit next 2 sts together; **mm** millimetre(s); **p** purl; **patt** pattern; **rem** remain(ing); **rep** repeat; **RS** right side; **st(s)** stitch(es); **st-st** stocking/ stockinette stitch; **WS** wrong side; **yo (yarn over needle)** take yarn over right needle to make a st

note

When working from chart, use separate small balls of yarn for each colour area and twist yarns at colour change to avoid holes.

back

With 3¾mm(US 5) needles and M, cast on 64(72:80) sts.

Working in st-st, beg with a k row and using intarsia method, rep the 42-row patt from the chart throughout, working between the lines for correct size and garment piece.

Cont until work measures 17(21:24)cm/6¾(8¼:9½)in, ending with a p row.

shape armhole

Cast/bind off 4 sts beg next 2 rows.

Cont without shaping until back measures 30.5(35.5:39.5)cm/12(14:15½) in, ending with a p row.

Note patt row.

shape shoulders and neck

1st row Cast/bind off 8(9:11) sts, patt 11(13:14), cast/bind off 18(20:22) sts, patt to end.

Work on this last set of sts.

2nd row Cast/bind off 8(9:11) sts, patt to end.

3rd row Cast/bind off 3 sts, patt to end.

4th row Cast/bind off.

Rejoin yarn at neck edge of first set of sts and work 3rd and 4th rows.

left front

With 3¾mm(US 5) needles and M, cast on 32(36:40) sts.

Working in st-st, beg with a k row and using intarsia method, rep the 42-row patt from the chart throughout, working between the lines for correct size and garment piece.

Cont until work measures 17(21:24)cm/6¾(8¼:9½)in, ending with a p row.

Shape armhole

Cast/bind off 4 sts, patt to end

Cont without shaping until 15(15:17) rows less have been worked than noted patt row for shoulder shaping, so ending with a k row.

shape neck

1st row (WS) cast/bind off 5(6:6) sts, patt to end.

2nd–4th rows Cont in patt dec 1 st at neck edge.

5th row P.

Cont in patt dec 1 st at neck edge on next (6th) row

and foll alt rows until 16(19:22) sts rem.

Work 3 more rows.

shape shoulder

1st row (RS) Cast/bind off 8(9:11) sts, patt to end.

2nd row P.

Cast/bind off.

right front

Work as given for Left Front, reversing all shapings.

sleeves

With 3mm(US 2–3) needles and M, cast on 33(35:37) sts.

1st row *K1, p1, rep from * to last st, k1

Repeat 1st row six times more.

8th row As 1st row, inc 1 st at end of row. 34(36:38) sts.

Change to 3¾mm(US 5) needles and st-st.

Working in st-st, beg with a k row and using intarsia method, rep the 42-row patt from the chart throughout, working between the lines for correct size and garment piece, **while at the same time**, inc 1 st at each end of 3rd row and every foll 4th(6th:6th) row until 56(44:52) sts and then sizes 2 and 3 on every foll 4th row until 66(72) sts.

Cont without shaping until work measures 23(28:31)cm/9(11:12¼)in.

Cast/bind off.

PM at each end of 6th row from cast/bind off-edge.

button band

With 3mm(US 2–3) needles and M, cast on 6 sts.

1st row *K1, p1, rep from * to end.

2nd row *P1, p1, rep from * to end.

Cont in moss/seed st until band, when slightly stretched, fits from cast-on edge to neck of Left Front.

Break yarn and leave sts on safety pin.

Mark positions for 5 buttons, the first 1cm/¾in from cast-on edge, the fifth 1cm/¾in above button band in the neckband, the remaining 3 evenly spaced between.

Sew band to Right Front.

buttonhole band

Work as for Button Band, making buttonholes where marked.
Buttonhole row Moss/seed st 2 sts, k2tog, yo, moss/seed st 2 sts.
Do not break yarn.

neckband

Join shoulder seams. With RS facing, 3mm(US 2–3) needles and M, moss/seed st across buttonhole band, pick up and k 20(20:22) sts from right front neck, 24(26:28) sts from back neck, 20(20:22) sts from left front neck, then moss/seed st across button band. 76(78:84) sts.
Work 5 rows in moss/seed st, making last buttonhole in 2nd row.

edging

With 3mm(US 2–3) needles and M, cast on 2 sts.
1st row Inc in 1st st, k1. 3 sts.
2nd row K1, p1, inc in last st. 4 sts.
3rd row Inc in 1st st, k1, p1, k1. 5 sts.
4th row [K1, p1] twice, inc in last st. 6 sts.
5th row Moss/seed st without shaping.
6th–9th rows Moss/seed st, dec 1 st at shaped edge on every row. 2 sts.
10th row K2.
Rep 1st–10th rows until straight edge fits lower edge of garment, excluding front bands, finishing with a 9th row before cast/bind off.

to finish

With centre cast/bound-off edge of sleeve to shoulder, sew sleeves into armholes with row ends above markers sewn to cast/bound-off sts at underarm. Join side and sleeve seams. Sew on buttons to correspond with buttonholes.

key
■ M
□ A

polka dot chart

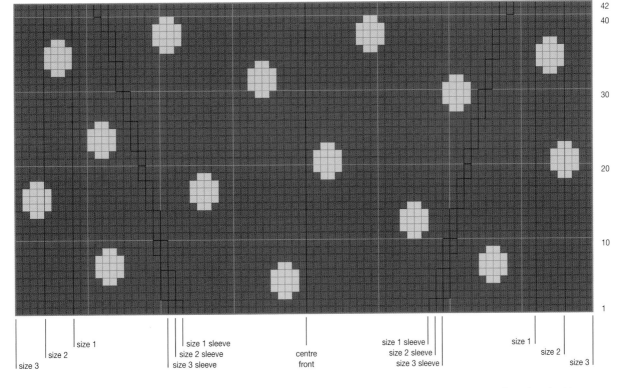

useful information

knitting abbreviations

The following are the general abbreviations used in the patterns. Special abbreviations are given with the individual patterns.

alt alternate

beg begin(ning)

cm centimetre(s)

cont continu(e)(ing)

cont straight continu(e)(ing) without shaping

dec decreas(e)(ing)

foll follow(s)(ing)

g gram(s)

g-st gram(s)

in inch(es)

inc increas(e)(ing)

k knit

kfb k into front and back of next st to inc one st

kp knit then purl into next st

m metre(s)

m1 make one st by picking up and working into back of loop between last st and next st

mm millimetre(s)

oz ounce(s)

p purl

patt pattern

pfb p into front and back of next st to inc one st

pk purl then knit into next st

psso pass slipped stitch over

rem remain(s)(ing)

rep repeat(s)(ing)

RS right side

skpo slip 1, k1, pass slipped st over

sk2togpo slip 1, k2tog, pass slipped st over

sl slip

ssk slip 1 knitwise, slip 1 knitwise, insert tip of left needle into fronts of 2 slipped sts and k2tog tbl

st(s) stitch(es)

st-st stocking/stockinette stitch

tbl through back of loop(s)

tog together

WS wrong side

yd yard(s)

yf yarn forward – bring yarn forward between needles and over right needle to make a st

yo (yon) yarn over needle – take yarn over right needle to make a st

yrn yarn round needle – wrap yarn around right needle from front to back and bring it to front again between needles to make a st

* repeat instructions after asterisk or between asterisks as many times as instructed

[ ] repeat instructions inside [ ]s as many times as instructed

substituting yarns

Knitting patterns always specify a particular brand of yarn. If you decide to use an alternative yarn be sure to calculate the number of balls or hanks you need by the metre (yard) rather than by the yarn weight. If you want to use a different yarn to the one suggested then match the shade as closely as possible.

yarn conversion chart

To convert	multiply by
grams to ounces	0.0352
ounces to grams	28.35
centimetres to inches	0.3937
inches to centimetres	2.54
metres to yards	0.9144
yards to metres	1.0936

UK and US knitting terminology

Most terms used in UK and US knitting patterns are the same, but a few are different. Where terms are different, they appear in the instructions divided by a /.

UK	US
cast off	bind off
moss stitch	seed stitch
stocking stitch	stockinette stitch
tension (size of stitch)	gauge
yarn over needle	yarn over (yo)
yarn forward	yarn over (yo)
yarn round needle	yarn over (yo)

suppliers

Rowan Yarns
Green Lane Mill, Holmfirth
West Yorkshire, HD7 1RW
01484 681881
www.rowanyarns.co.uk

Jaeger Yarns
As Rowan
01484 680050

knitting needle conversion chart

This chart shows you how the different knitting needle-size systems compare.

Metric	US sizes	Old UK
2mm	0	14
2¼mm	1	13
2¾mm	2	12
3mm		11
3¼mm	3	10
3¾mm	5	9
4mm	6	8
4½mm	7	7
5mm	8	6
5½mm	9	5
6mm	10	4
6½mm	10½	3
7mm	10½	2
7½mm	11	1
8mm	11	0
9mm	13	00
10mm	15	000

index

acknowledgements

author acknowledgements

Thank you to all the fabulous knitters, especially Mandy and Eva, for their beautiful knitting. Also, a big thank you to Rosy for helping me with the pattern checking. Thank you to Rozelle and Adrian for their sense of style and great photos which bring my designs to life. Last but not least, a big thank you to all the lovely models and their parents who came from near and far to be in this book – especially my own gorgeous two, Toby and Kitty, who have been great and have put up with such a busy mother!

publisher acknowledgements

The Publishers would like to thank Daniel Attwood, Louis Barnes-Jones, Lily Belle de la Mer, Charlotte Brown, Maysoon Collier, Natalie d'Enno, Owen Harris, Rumi Hugo-Fox, Lola Perrin, Neo Tanner, Minnie Venning, Lola Walters, Kitty Wynne-Mellor, Toby Wynne-Mellor for being such wonderful models. They would also like to thank Gordon and Sheila Pope and Zoë Mellor for the kind loan of their homes. Thanks also to the Bluebird Café in Goring, the flower stall in Hove, Hannah Goodman, Emma Hancox and Emily Wilkinson.

Executive Editor Sarah Tomley
Senior Editor Rachel Lawrence
Pattern Checker Pauline Hornsby
Executive Art Editor Rozelle Bentheim
Designer Beverly Price, one2six creative
Photographer Adrian Pope
Illustrator Kuo Kang Chen
Production Manager Manjit Sihra